Fair Money

This book explains how our monetary system really works and how commercial banks create money. The effects of this are examined, along with an alternate monetary system that is vastly superior – which we term Fair Money.

Poverty is not an accident. Like slavery and apartheid, it is man-made and can be removed by the actions of human beings.

- Nelson Mandela

Dedication

This book is dedicated to my mom and my dad (who did the best that they could in difficult times) and to my sister, who was taken away before her time.

To the readers of this book who sense that something is wrong with our monetary system; contained within the pages are the facts that you need to make sense of it all. But only by acting with such knowledge can you make a difference.

Disclaimer: None of the information in this book should be considered to be legal, financial or investment advice. If you need such advice, please seek the services of a registered professional.

Table of Contents

The term Fair Money originates from the
Australian slang "fair dinkum".

fair dinkum

adjective phrase

Honest; fair and just

Chapter 1 :   Playing Monopoly

The study of money, above all other fields in economics, is one in which complexity is used to disguise truth or to evade truth, not to reveal it.

John Kenneth Galbraith
Money: Whence it came, where it went
1975

Background

The game of Monopoly has its origin in 1904 when Elizabeth Magie patented a game entitled The Landlord's Game. A variation thereof, with the title Monopoly emerged during the 1930s and was marketed by the company Parker Brothers. As with many successful products, copyright and trademark claims appeared from numerous directions. The story of these claims and counterclaims makes for interesting reading, but they are not the subject of this book. Rather we will examine the game and its imitation of our current monetary system.

Rules and objective

The objective of Monopoly is to become the wealthiest player through the buying, renting and selling of properties. There are normally 28 properties available to be purchased at an average price of $200. Using the classic rules; the game is started after each player is **given** $1,500 of notes. The extract of this rule is below:

Each player is given $1,500 divided as follows: 2 each of $500s, $100s and $50s; 6 $20s; 5 each of $10s, $5s and $1s.

There are rules regarding the purchase and sale of properties, the collection of rent and the payment of income taxes. The game also allows for each player to be paid a salary of $200 each time they pass over the square labelled GO:

"GO": Each time a player's token lands on or passes over GO, whether by throwing the dice or drawing a card, the Banker pays him/her a $200 salary.

Playing the game

Monopoly seems to be a fair reflection of our economic reality; as there are random events that can occur (i.e. by throwing the dice), properties are bought or sold, income taxes are paid and salaries are received. Each player has the opportunity to acquire wealth (i.e. properties and cash) while the possibility exists that they may become bankrupt.

The banker is essentially an outsider, and not involved in the quest of accumulating wealth. By virtue of not being a player; the banker can never be a winner. To an independent observer this seems to be a sensible arrangement.

Closer to reality

However, there are two major differences between the game of Monopoly and the real world. These differences are:

- In the classic rules, the bank **gives** each player $1,500 at the start of the game. In the real world, banks only **lend** money – they never give money to the public as part of their normal business.

- In the classic rules, each player receives $200 from the bank as they pass GO. In the real world, the overwhelming majority of people do not receive a salary from a bank.

To bring the game into alignment with reality; we make two amendments to the existing rules. The first change is that of replacing a single word in the classic rules (as highlighted below):

> Each player is **lent** $1,500 divided as follows: 2 each of $500s, $100s and $50s; 6 $20s; 5 each of $10s, $5s and $1s.

The second change is that of removing the rule that requires the bank to pay each player $200 when they pass over the square labelled GO. With these changes in place – we resume the game.

Debt servitude

The classic rules require that the bank charge 10% on any mortgage. To remain consistent, we apply the same rate to the bank loans. Similar to a mortgage, each player must repay their loan with interest. In this case, we require 10 equal repayments; with each repayment made as the player makes a complete navigation around the board. Using a calculator, we find that each repayment is $244, resulting in total repayments of $2,440.

Assume there are 3 players in the game (plus the banker). At the start of the game, the banker **lends** a total of $4,500 to the three players. At this point, all the cash is in the hands of the players.

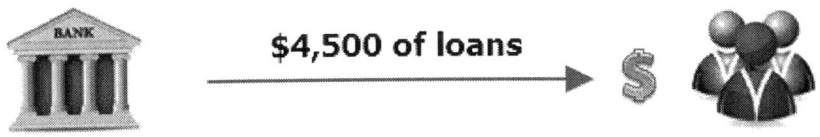

As the game progresses, each player makes repayments to the bank. Once the slowest player has completed 10 rounds, the situation is as followings:

 **$4,500 has been repaid**

$2,820 Debt

All the cash is back in the hands of the bank, leaving the players with a collective debt of $2,820. This figure is calculated as follows:

$$\text{Debt } \$2,820 = 3 \text{ players x } (\$2,440 - \$1,500)$$

If the players want to continue playing the game, they have to apply at the bank for new loans, thereby exacerbating their indebtedness.

The strongest player

By changing two rules in the game of Monopoly (so that it aligns with reality) results in the transformation of the bank from a neutral party into the strongest player on the board. Moreover, the bank does not roll the dice and is not even involved in the primary activity of the game, i.e. the buying of property for the purpose of collecting rent.

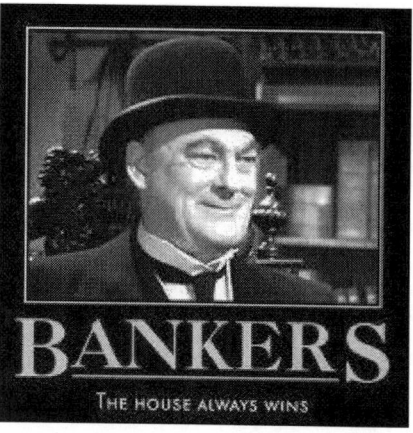

It should be clear that in a game of Monopoly where the bank **lends money into circulation,** the end result is the transfer of wealth from the players to the bank. The more time is spent playing the game; the greater is the certainty and quantum of wealth transferred.

A global game

The middle class of developed nations are unwitting participants in a real life game of Monopoly; where money is created and lent into circulation, and where the rules of the game are opaque and mysterious. Throughout the industrialised world, private and public sectors are burdened with unpayable levels of debt; with financial austerity touted as the only remedy.

It is interesting to note that one of the rules from the British version of Monopoly states the following:

> The Bank never "goes bankrupt" but can issue as much money as is necessary in the form of IOUs written on ordinary paper.

Compare this rule with the quote from the past Governor of the Central Bank of Canada (as given below).

 Broadly speaking, **all new money comes out of a Bank in the form of loans**... As loans are debts, then under the present system all money is debt.

Graham F. Towers
Past Governor of the Central Bank of Canada
(from 1934 to 1955)

Perhaps this one rule expresses the true nature of our current monetary system. To find out if this is the case, keep reading...

KEEP READING ↓

Chapter 2 :   Bank of England

Whenever a bank makes a loan, it simultaneously creates a matching deposit in the borrower's bank account, thereby creating new money.

Bank of England
March 2014

Lifting the veil

On 12 March 2014 the veil that concealed the inner mechanism of commercial and central banking was lifted by none other than the Bank of England. Their First Quarterly Bulletin for 2014 contains two articles which has triggered a tectonic shift in the debate on money and banking. The two articles are:

- Money in the modern economy: an introduction.
- Money creation in the modern economy.

Both articles are discussed further below.

Tweets

On the same day the Bank of England posted the following tweet:

Bank of England ✓
@bankofengland

In the modern economy, money is mostly created by banks making loans ow.ly/uuTiF

A short while later they posted a second tweet:

Bank of England ✅
@bankofengland

97% of broad money takes the form of bank deposits – which are created by commercial banks ow.ly/uuTvN

The second tweet is unambiguous in its message, and provides us with the following information:

- Of the broad money measure; 97% is commercial bank deposits.
- All commercial bank deposits are created by the banks.

These tweets are a superb summation of the two published articles. In support of their position, the Bank of England even provides a list of 44 references at the end of the article; Money creation in the modern economy. Students on the subject are encouraged to locate these articles and familiarise themselves with the contents thereof.

 Most of the money in circulation is created, not by the printing presses of the Bank of England, but by the commercial banks themselves: **banks create money whenever they lend to someone in the economy** or buy an asset from consumers.

Bank of England
First Quarterly Bulletin 2014

Intermediation

For decades the banking industry contested the notion that commercial banks create money. Even to this day, academia and the media continue to promote the idea that banks act as intermediaries. On this subject, the Bank of England states:

> One common misconception is that banks act simply as intermediaries, lending out the deposits that savers place with them.

The Bank continues and states in the most concise manner:

> **Commercial banks create money, in the form of bank deposits, by making new loans.**

A subsequent chapter in this book is dedicated to the process whereby commercial banks create money. This mechanism is called debt monetisation, and is employed by both commercial banks and central banks. In a nutshell; commercial banks are not intermediaries between lenders and borrowers. They create all the money required by borrowers and they leave the deposits of existing clients untouched.

 When banks make loans, they create additional deposits for those that have borrowed the money.

Bank of England
Monetary Analysis Division
2007

The money multiplier

Students of finance are taught that money is somehow multiplied at the commercial bank level, and that this takes place with reference to some nominal quantity of reserves held at a central bank. The Bank of England destroys this cherished notion when it states:

> Another common misconception is that the central bank determines the quantity of loans and deposits in the economy by controlling the quantity of central bank money - the so-called "money multiplier" approach.

The statement below from the Bank of England on the use of the money multiplier should be reason enough for whole chapters in prestigious textbooks to be expunged:

> While the money multiplier theory can be a useful way of introducing money and banking in economic textbooks, **it is not an accurate description of how money is created** in reality.

The Bank then repeats itself in succinct manner.

> In normal times, the central bank does not fix the amount of money in circulation, nor is central bank money "multiplied up" into more loans and deposits.

It is safe to conclude that the money multiplier has no relevance in our modern economy.

Lending affects reserves

Reserves are generally understood to be the deposits that commercial banks maintain at their central bank. Textbooks describe a mechanism whereby these reserves are referenced when commercial banks calculate how much money they can lend. The Bank of England refutes this notion when it states:

> In no way does the aggregate quantity of reserves directly constrain the amount of bank lending or deposit creation.

The Bank points out that the mechanism works in the opposite manner:

> The relationship between reserves and loans typically operates in the reverse way to that described in some economics textbooks.

The Bank concludes by explaining how the mechanism actually works:

> The amount of [commercial] bank deposits in turn influences how much central bank money [the commercial] banks want to hold in reserve (to meet withdrawals by the public, make payments to other banks, or meet regulatory liquidity requirements).

The belief that central bank reserves constrain commercial bank lending, is incorrect. Commercial bank lending affects central bank reserves.

Lending reserves

In Australia reserve accounts are called Exchange Settlement accounts and they are held at the Reserve Bank of Australia. The Bank of England provides a succinct explanation of what reserve accounts are used for:

> A related misconception is that banks can lend out their reserves. Reserves can only be lent between banks, since consumers do not have access to reserves accounts at the Bank of England.

A common and erroneous refrain from market commentators is that commercial banks can access surplus reserves and then lend the money to the general public. Such statements are made by pundits who fail to grasp the fact that reserves only move between reserve accounts, and cannot be lent to the public.

 Banks can't "do" anything with all the extra reserve balances. Loans create deposits - reserve balances don't finance lending or add any "fuel" to the economy.

Professor Scott Fullwiler

A subsequent chapter explains how reserve accounts work.

Summary

The two articles from the Bank of England overturn many cherished beliefs held by the public. The Bank points out in clear language that:

- Commercial banks create money.
- Commercial banks are not intermediaries.
- The money multiplier has no application in the real world.
- Reserve accounts do not constrain commercial bank lending.
- Excess reserves are not lent to the general public.

The articles should result in swathes of text books being withdrawn and republished with updated chapters. The reality is that this is unlikely to occur in the foreseeable future.

 Economics is haunted by more fallacies than any other study known to man.

Henry Hazlitt (1894 – 1993)
American journalist
The Wall Street Journal and The New York Times

Chapter 3 :   International Monetary Fund

Bank liabilities are money that can be created and destroyed at a moment's notice. The critical importance of this fact appears to have been lost in much of the modern macroeconomics literature on banking.

The International Monetary Fund
August 2012

Intermediation

In August 2012 the Research Department of the International Monetary Fund published a document entitled The Chicago Plan Revisited. The document examines the history of government issued money, including a proposal for monetary reform made prior to World War II by leading economists in the United States. The proposal calls for the separation of government and banking functions; in that the government should create all the money in circulation and that the banking sector should only lend out existing money.

The Chicago Plan

The proposal was originally floated in 1936 and was named The Chicago Plan. The name emanates from the fact that its strongest advocate was Professor Henry Simons from the University of Chicago. An enthusiastic supporter of the proposal was Irving Fisher of Yale University, and many of the public statements surrounding the plan came from his pen and pronouncements.

The proposal in The Chicago Plan is that the government should create and issue all money, while commercial banks only lend existing money that is deposited with them. Under such an arrangement, commercial banks become true intermediaries between lenders and borrowers, and are not able to create money (as is the case today).

Benefits

Irving Fisher claims that if The Chicago Plan is implemented at the national level, the following conditions will materialise:

- Boom and bust business cycles will be tempered.
- Banks runs will be completely eliminated.
- Government debt will be dramatically reduced.
- Private debt will be dramatically reduced.

These are lofty claims, and if accurate one can imagine sovereign governments (i.e. governments acting in the interest of their citizens) implementing the plan post-haste. In the abstract of the document, the IMF states:

> We find support for all four of Fisher's claims. Furthermore, output gains approach 10%, and steady state inflation can drop to zero without posing problems for the conduct of monetary policy.

An output gain of 10% refers to an increase in gross domestic product. What is astonishing is that in the summary the IMF goes further and states:

> We find that the advantages of The Chicago Plan go even beyond those claimed by Fisher. One additional advantage is large steady state output gains due to the removal or reduction of multiple distortions, including interest rate risk spreads, distortionary taxes, and costly monitoring of macro economically unnecessary credit risks. Another advantage is the ability to **drive steady state inflation to zero...**

To support their conclusions, the IMF includes a chapter where they detail the mathematics used to model our current monetary system and the monetary system proposed in The Chicago Plan.

Choose

To encapsulate the conclusions of the International Monetary Fund; if the government creates all the money in circulation, then:

- Government and private debt will be reduced.
- GDP will increase 10%.
- Taxes will be reduced.
- Price inflation will be driven to zero.

The conditions described above are significantly better than the pallid conditions that exist in most developed economies. If the public were given the opportunity to select one of the options below - their selection would be easy to predict.

Current system	The Chicago Plan
High government debt	Low government debt
High personal debt	Low personal debt
High taxes	Low taxes
Current GDP level	GDP raised by 10%
High price inflation	Zero price inflation
Possibility of bank runs	No bank runs
Disruptive business cycles	Smoothed business cycles

The International Monetary Fund states that the reason The Chicago Plan was never adopted in the United States, is due to "strong resistance from the banking industry".

Money multiplier

The International Monetary Fund not only corroborates the statements by the Bank of England regarding the money multiplier, but they go further and call it a myth:

> Reserves therefore impose no constraint. The **deposit multiplier** is simply, in the words of Kydland and Prescott (1990), a **myth**. And because of this, private banks are almost fully in control of the money creation process.

The Federal Reserve Board (Washington D.C.) published an article dated May 2010 with the title Money, Reserves, and the Transmission of Monetary Policy: Does the Money Multiplier Exist? In the article they state the following:

> Simple textbook treatments of the money multiplier give the quantity of bank reserves a causal role in determining the quantity of money and bank lending and thus the transmission mechanism of monetary policy. This role results from the assumptions that reserve requirements generate a direct and tight linkage between money and reserves and that the central bank controls the money supply by adjusting the quantity of reserves through open market operations. Using data from recent decades, we have demonstrated that **this simple textbook link is implausible** in the United States ...

Three financial institutions; the Bank of England, the International Monetary Fund and the Federal Reserve Board, state that the money multiplier is irrelevant in our current monetary system.

Government issued money

The Chicago Plan Revisited includes a thought provoking chapter on the history of private and government issued money. A few selected statements from the document are reproduced below:

The historical debate concerning the nature and control of money is the subject of Zarlenga (2002), a masterful work that traces this debate back to ancient Mesopotamia, Greece and Rome. Like Graeber (2011), he shows that **private issuance of money has repeatedly led to major societal problems throughout recorded history**, due to usury associated with private debts.

Regarding Solon (638 BC – 558 BC) as an Athenian lawmaker:

Solon provided much more plentiful government-issued, debt-free coinage that reduced the need for private debts. Solon's reforms were so successful that, 150 years later, the early Roman republic sent a delegation to Greece to study them. **They became the foundation of the Roman monetary system from 454 BC**.

Regarding Aristotle and his view of money:

In *Ethics*, Aristotle clearly states the state/institutional theory of money, and rejects any commodity-based or trading concept of money, by saying **"Money exists not by nature but by law."**

The International Monetary Fund also examined the history of the United Kingdom, and made a number of statements contrary to popular belief:

The results for the United Kingdom are quite clear. Shaw (1896) examined the record of monarchs throughout English history, and found that, with one exception (Henry VIII), the king had used his monetary prerogative responsibly for the benefit of the nation, **with no major financial crises**.

On the issue of backing money with gold or silver, the International Monetary Fund states:

> The one blemish on the record of government money issuance was deflationary rather than inflationary in nature. The van Buren presidency [eighth President of the United States (1837–1841)] triggered the 1837 depression by insisting that the government issuance of money had a 100% gold/silver backing. **This completely unnecessary straitjacket meant that the money supply was inadequate for a growing economy.**

The Governor

The proposal in The Chicago Plan can improve the lives of billions of people. However, the article from the International Monetary Fund is not openly discussed in academia or in the media.

The ruinous state of our monetary system is best described by Mervyn Allister King. Mr King was the Deputy Governor at the Bank of England from 1998 to 2003, and the Governor and Chairman of its Monetary Policy Committee from 2003 to 2013.

 Of all the many ways of organising banking, the worst is the one we have today.

Mervyn Allister King

Chapter 4 :   The Guernsey experiment

The experiments continued over a period of 20 years, by which time the people of Guernsey had developed from a depressed unhappy state to a position of prosperity and happiness.

Edward Holloway
How Guernsey beat the bankers
1981

Island of Guernsey

Guernsey is an island that is physically situated in the English Channel (between France and England) and is a possession of the British Crown. The States of Guernsey is the parliament of the Isle of Guernsey, and consists of 45 elected representatives from various districts.

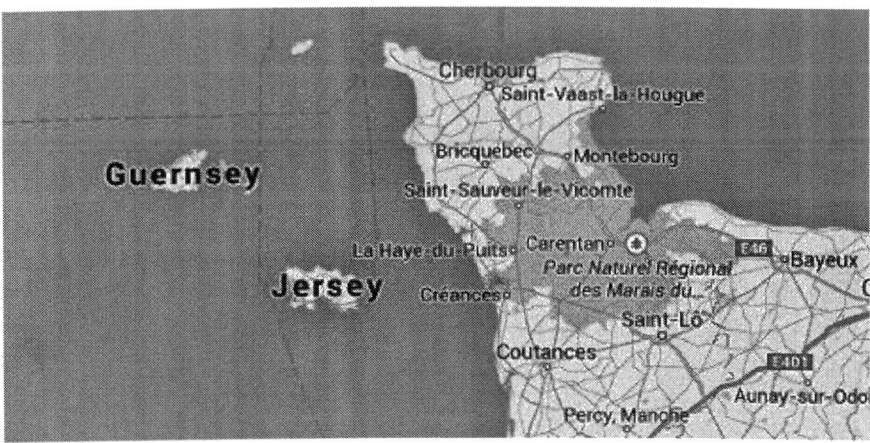

After the Napoleonic wars ended in 1815, the island found itself in dire financial straits, with little or no trade and limited employment opportunities. The infrastructure on the island, such as the roads, were in an appalling state and the sea threatened to overflow large parts of the island due to the sea walls being inadequate.

A committee was appointed to examine the issue, and came to the conclusion that it would be impossible to further tax the population for the necessary funds. The governor at the time suggested that the States of Guernsey exercise its sovereign prerogative and produce its own notes in order to finance the required reconstruction.

Prosperity

Between the years 1819 and 1836 the state produced its own notes and thereby financed the construction of roads, the building of a sea wall, the rebuilding of Elizabeth College (which had been founded by Queen Elizabeth in 1563) and numerous other public works. The States of Guernsey took great care in determining the quantity of notes issued, so as not to flood its economy with new notes.

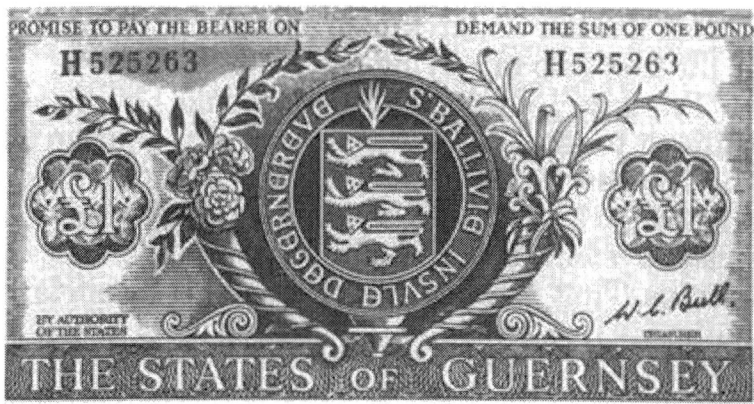

During this period, all public works were undertaken without any increase in the public debt. One would assume that this would be to the liking of all residents on the island, since Guernsey developed from a depressed island into one of general prosperity. Alas, this was not the case. From the booklet entitled How Guernsey Beat the Bankers, we learn the following:

> But this happy state of affairs was not to the liking of everyone, and opposition to the idea of the Island States creating their own "debt-free" money had been growing over the years, particularly among the banking interests on the island.

Capitulation

In 1830 the banks struck their first blow with the establishment of the Commercial Bank, which issued its own notes and soon flooded the island with paper money. The matter came to a head in September 1836, when Daniel de Lisle Brock made a spirited speech at a meeting of the States of Guernsey where he said:

> No one has a right to arrogate to himself the power of circulating a private coinage on which he imprints for his own profit an arbitrary value.
>
> With these facts before our eyes we must realise that necessity of limiting the issue of paper money to the needs and customs, and the benefit, of the community in general. Permission cannot be granted to certain individuals to play with the wealth and prosperity of society.

What followed is not on the public record, apart from letters between bank representatives and the Bailiff of the Island, where the bank representatives suggest that the States of Guernsey should cease issuing further notes and withdraw existing notes. The Bailiff agreed, and so in 1836 the Guernsey experiment ceased.

In this short tale lies a harsh and salutary lesson for mankind.

KEEP READING

Chapter 5 :   Debt monetisation

So you think that money is the root of all evil. Have
you ever asked what is the root of all money?

Ayn Rand

Banks create money

The Bank of England has answered in emphatic fashion the question of who
creates the money we use in the economy. On the question of **how** money
is created; the Bank of England states that when commercial banks make a
loan they simultaneously create a deposit.

 In the modern economy, most money takes the form of bank
deposits. But how those bank deposits are created is often
misunderstood: the principal way is through commercial
banks making loans. **Whenever a bank makes a loan, it
simultaneously creates a matching deposit** in the
borrower's bank account, thereby creating new money.

Money in the modern economy
The Bank of England
2014

The quote above begs a detailed explanation, especially for those who have
an interest in banking and finance. This chapter provides that explanation,
even to those who have a limited grasp of accounting.

At this point some clarification is required. Subsequent chapters show that
the Australian dollar exists in numerous forms, with each form created by a
different party. This chapter deals only with digital money created by
commercial banks.

Journal entry

The concept of how digital money is created is so simple, that this should be the shortest chapter. We start by examining the Annual Report of the ANZ Bank for 2014. The largest number on the asset side of their balance sheet is **Net loans and advances**.

		Consolidated	
	Note	2014 $m	2013[1] $m
Assets			
Cash	9	32,559	25,270
Settlement balances owed to ANZ		20,241	19,225
Collateral paid		5,459	6,530
Trading securities	10	49,692	41,288
Derivative financial instruments	11	56,369	45,878
Available-for-sale assets	12	30,917	28,277
Net loans and advances	13	521,752	483,264
Regulatory deposits		1,565	2,106

The largest number on the liability side of their balance sheet is **Deposits and other borrowings**.

Liabilities			
Settlement balances owed by ANZ		10,114	8,695
Collateral received		5,599	3,921
Deposits and other borrowings	21	510,079	466,915
Derivative financial instruments	11	52,925	47,509

Recall the use of the words **loan** and **deposit** by the Bank of England. These are the two categories affected when commercial banks create money. When a person applies for and receives a loan, they have at least two accounts at the bank, i.e.

- A deposit account (where the new money is placed).
- A loan account (which records their obligation to the bank).

We now examine the journal entry posted by commercial banks when they advance a loan. Assume Mr Jones applies for a loan of $500,000 and that the bank agrees. Once the legal documents are signed, the bank posts the entry below:

Commercial Bank – Journal			
	Account	Debits	Credits
Dr	Loan – Mr Jones	$500,000	
Cr	Deposit - Mr Jones		$500,000

This is it. This is how banks create digital money. This is the accounting entry at the core of our modern banking system. It is the simplicity of this process that leaves so many people bewildered. Once this concept is assimilated, the statement by Professor Galbraith becomes clear.

 The study of money, above all other fields in economics, is one in which complexity is used to disguise truth or to evade truth, not to reveal it. **The process by which banks create money is so simple the mind is repelled.**

Professor John Kenneth Galbraith
Former Professor of Economics at Harvard
Money: Whence it came, where it went (1975)

Balance sheet

When the journal entry is posted to the general ledger, it increases the loans at the bank by $500,000 and simultaneously increases the deposits at the bank by $500,000. This mechanism is called debt monetisation.

Commercial Bank – Balance Sheet			
Assets		Liabilities	
Loan – Mr Jones	$500,000	Deposit – Mr Jones	$500,000
		New money	

The Bank of England confirms that existing deposits are not affected when commercial banks make loans.

 Rather than banks' lending out deposits that are placed with them, **the act of lending creates deposits** — the reverse of the sequence typically described in textbooks

Bank of England
Money creation in the modern economy
First Quarterly Bulletin 2014

Debts and profits

Commercial banks operate to maximise their profit. Since the largest contributor to their profit is interest earned from loans; commercial banks are

 inexorably driven to increase the quantum of their loans. This quest is expressed in the media with statements to the effect that banks needs to **grow their assets**. The term "assets" refer to the loans that appear on the asset side of their balance sheet.

It is no stretch to conclude that the level of societal debt is merely the collateral damage that follows in the wake of banks striving for ever higher levels of profit.

Debt demonetisation

When commercial banks monetise debt; the quantity of commercial bank money in the economy increases. When a borrower repays a portion of their loan, the bank destroys existing commercial bank money. This reduces the supply of money in the economy.

With reference to the balance sheet above; if Mr Jones repays $50,000 of his loan, the bank posts the following journal entry.

Commercial Bank – Journal			
	Account	Debits	Credits
Dr	Deposit – Mr Jones	$50,000	
Cr	Loan – Mr Jones		$50,000

The balance sheet of the bank now looks as follows:

Commercial Bank – Balance Sheet			
Assets		Liabilities	
Loan – Mr Jones	$450,000	Deposit – Mr Jones	$450,000
		Money supply is reduced	

Understanding this simple mechanism of how commercial banks create new money (when making a loan) and destroy existing money (when a loan is repaid) is crucial to quantifying the financial benefit inherent in the Fair Money solution.

In Australia, the application of the Fair Money solution can result in approximately $1.827 trillion of new money being created and spent into circulation on infrastructure without any impact on monetary inflation or price inflation. Similar benefits are available to countries that adopt the Fair Money solution. The issue is discussed in detail in a subsequent chapter.

Terminology

Throughout the remainder of this book, the terms debt monetisation and monetising debt are used interchangeably; since they mean the same thing.

 Do private banks issue money today? Yes. Although banks no longer have the right to issue bank notes, they can create money in the form of bank deposits when they lend money to businesses, or buy securities... **When banks lend money they don't necessarily take it from anyone else to lend.** Thus they create it.

US Congressman Wright Patman
House Committee on Banking and Currency
1964

Chapter 6 :   From gold to fiat

All the perplexities, confusion and distresses in America arise not from defects in the constitution or confederation, nor from want of honour or virtue, as much from downright ignorance of the nature of coin, credit, and circulation.

John Adams
In a letter to Thomas Jefferson

Bank runs

In the early 20th century, commercial bank notes and Australian notes (issued by the Treasurer of the Commonwealth of Australia) were convertible into gold and silver coins. The quest of commercial banks for greater profit propelled them to issue ever greater numbers of bank notes relative to their holding of precious metals, while banking regulations provided only a gentle restraint on such expansion.

The risk that each commercial bank faced was that of a bank run; where clients would demand the bank meet its legal obligation to **pay gold on demand**. This demand could be issued by holders of bank notes or by clients who had funds in their bank account.

In the United States, bank runs were not only visible (as evident in the picture above), but once rumour and speculation took hold, it had the power to close down any commercial bank within a day or two.

Epochs

This chapter provides a glimpse of the pivotal points in history that have shaped our monetary landscape and the reporting changes that ensued. This chapter is not a substitute for some of the outstanding books on the subject, such as The Lost Science of Money by Stephen Zarlenga. The objective is to provide a brief sketch of the de-monetisation of gold and silver. The epochs that are discussed are:

- Commercial bank notes.
- Debt monetisation.
- Central bank notes.
- End of convertibility.

Commercial bank notes

During the time that gold and silver coins were considered to be money, commercial banks issued bank promissory notes (called bank notes) as evidence of their liability to exchange the note for precious metals. A typical bank note for £2 Sterling is given below:

As an example, assume that a member of the public deposits some gold coins with a face value of £1,000 at the bank, and requests a bank note in return. Once the bank note is issued, the bank balance sheet looks as follows:

Commercial Bank – Balance Sheet			
Assets		Liabilities	
Gold coins	£1,000	Bank notes	£1,000

Assume Mr Jenkins deposits his gold coins with a face value of £1,000 at the bank, but requests that the bank credit his personal account. The bank balance sheet will now look as follows:

Commercial Bank – Balance Sheet			
Assets		Liabilities	
Gold coins	£2,000	Bank notes	£1,000
		Deposit – Mr Jenkins	£1,000

Note that the gold coins are recorded as being an asset of the bank (i.e. the commercial bank actually owns the coins) while Mr Jenkins has a claim against the bank for the value of the coins. In the case of the bank note; whoever holds the promissory note has a claim against the bank for the value of the coins.

Debt monetisation

With the growth of commercial banks came their desire to maximise profit. In 1961 the Federal Reserve Bank of Chicago published the book Modern Money Mechanics. The book describes how commercial banks create money, even while operating under the gold standard:

It started with goldsmiths. As early bankers, they initially provided safekeeping services, making a profit from vault storage fees for gold and coins deposited with them. People would redeem their "deposit receipts" whenever they needed gold or coins to purchase something, and physically take the gold or coins to the seller who, in turn, would deposit them for safekeeping, often with the same banker. Everyone soon found that **it was a lot easier simply to use the deposit receipts directly as a means of payment.** These receipts, which became known as notes, were acceptable as money since whoever held them could go to the banker and exchange them for metallic money.

Then, bankers discovered that they could make loans merely by giving their promises to pay, or bank notes, to borrowers. In this way, **banks began to create money.** More notes could be issued than the gold and coin on hand because only a portion of the notes outstanding would be presented for payment at any one time.

Returning to our example; assume Mr Green applies for a loan of £2,000 from the bank. Once approved, the bank balance sheet looks as follows:

Commercial Bank – Balance Sheet			
Assets		Liabilities	
Gold coins	£2,000	Bank notes	£1,000
		Deposit – Mr Jenkins	£1,000
Loan – Mr Green	£2,000	Deposit – Mr Green	£2,000
New asset		**New money**	

This last transaction is identical to the transaction that modern commercial banks post when they advance a loan (i.e. when they monetise a debt). It should be obvious that debt monetisation is not a modern banking phenomenon, but was common banking practice during the gold standard.

Central bank notes

In the early 1900s the monetary landscape in Australia changed irrevocably. The milestones that marked these changes are:

- In 1911 the Commonwealth Bank Act established the Commonwealth Bank of Australia.
- In 1920 the Commonwealth Bank Act was amended to give the Commonwealth Bank control over the issuance of Australian notes, which previously vested with the Australian Treasury.
- In 1924 the Commonwealth Bank Act was amended and the Commonwealth Bank was given authority to issue Australian notes to other banks.

The last amendment altered the way commercial banks operate, and how they structured their balance sheets. Section 18 of this amendment states:

> The Board may issue Australian notes to the [Commonwealth] Bank or to other banks in Australia in exchange for money or securities lodged with the London branch of the [Commonwealth] Bank.

The amendment allowed commercial banks to replace gold and silver coins in their vaults with Australian notes. During this time, the Commonwealth Bank was owned by the government of Australia, making it the de facto central bank. Commercial banks readily adopted this new practice, due to the cost saving and the public perception that Australian notes were more secure than commercial bank notes.

Replace gold with Australian notes

The process whereby Australian notes replaced precious metal coins, and the reporting thereof, can be described as a two-step process. The first step occurred when commercial banks lodged their precious metals at the Commonwealth Bank in London and received Australian notes. In our example, the bank replaced £2,000 of gold coins with Australian notes.

Commercial Bank – Balance Sheet			
Assets		Liabilities	
Australian notes	£2,000	Bank notes	£1,000
		Deposit – Mr Jenkins	£1,000
Loan – Mr Green	£2,000	Deposit – Mr Green	£2,000
Replace gold with notes			

Cancel bank notes

The second step occurred as members of the public who held bank notes, approached their local bank and requested Australian notes. Commercial banks accepted the notes, cancelled them and then handed over Australian notes with the same face value.

In our example, the public presented £1,000 of bank notes. The bank accepted the notes, cancelled them and handed over £1,000 of Australian notes. Once done, their balance sheet looked as follows:

Commercial Bank – Balance Sheet			
Assets		Liabilities	
Australian notes	£1,000	Bank notes	-
		Deposit – Mr Jenkins	£1,000
Loan – Mr Green	£2,000	Deposit – Mr Green	£2,000
Public exchange bank notes for Australian notes			

This balance sheet structure (albeit a simplification) is what modern commercial bank balance sheets look like. A subsequent chapter examines bank balance sheets in greater detail.

End of convertibility

The Commonwealth Bank Act of 1932 removed the link between Australian notes and precious metals. Holders of Australian notes for amounts of one pound and under, had 20 years from the date of issue to redeem their notes, while those with Australian notes for amounts of greater than one pound, had 40 years from the date of issue to redeem their notes.

Fiat money

The legislation favourably affected the Commonwealth Bank, since it was the issuer of Australian notes at the time. Any gold or silver not claimed by the public during the period of grace became part of the reserves of the bank.

In 1933 the Commonwealth Bank issued new Australian Notes. These notes were not backed by gold or silver, effectively rendering the money supply fiat. Fiat money is defined as follows:

> Fiat money is a currency established as money **by government regulation or law**. The term derives from the Latin fiat ("let it be done", "it shall be") used in the sense of an order or decree.
>
> In monetary economics, fiat money is an intrinsically useless object or record that is widely accepted as a means of payment.

Perception

It is interesting to observe the subtle change that occurred in public perception regarding money. Historically, gold and silver coins were considered to be money, and bank notes were claims against the bank for the return of such precious metals.

With the passage of time, bank notes and digital deposits become money, while precious metals are now classified as commodities (to be bought and sold) or reserves (to be held by central banks).

Chapter 7 :   Five money classes

It is well enough that people of the nation do not understand our banking and monetary system, for if they did, I believe there would be a revolution before tomorrow morning.

Henry Ford

Money classes

The next few chapters will elucidate the concept that there is not just one class of money in Australia, but that there are five different classes of money – regardless that each class is denominated in the Australian dollar.

Additionally, there is not just one party than creates the Australian dollar, or one mechanism whereby the dollar is introduced into circulation, or one segment of society that benefits when the dollar is created; but that there are numerous parties, numerous mechanisms and numerous beneficiaries involved in the creation of the Australian dollar.

In previous chapters where the term **banks create money** is used; such reference was only to a particular class of money, namely commercial bank money. As will become evident, it is not only commercial banks that create money, but that the Australian dollar is created by:

- The Perth Mint.
- The Royal Australian Mint.
- The Reserve Bank of Australia (the RBA).
- The commercial banks in Australia.

Below is a summation of the five money classes that exist, including the parties that create money and the parties that benefit from money creation:

Money class	Created by	Beneficiary
Currency coins	Royal Australian Mint	Commonwealth
Currency notes	Central bank	Central bank
Commercial bank money	Commercial banks	Commercial banks
Central bank money	Central bank	Central bank
Gold and silver coins	The Perth Mint The Royal Australian Mint	Commonwealth

Seigniorage

Understanding seigniorage is essential to understanding the benefits generated when money is created and placed into circulation. Investopedia has a good definition that is worth examining.

What is 'Seigniorage'

The difference between the value of money and the cost to produce it - in other words, the economic cost of producing a currency within a given economy or country. If the seigniorage is positive, then the government will make an economic profit; a negative seigniorage will result in an economic loss.

RBA statistics

The Reserve Bank of Australia provides statistics regarding money used in the economy and at the central bank level. The statistics can be found in the Monetary Aggregates spread sheet on their web site. The Reserve Bank uses the following money categories:

- Currency (i.e. notes and coins).
- Deposits at banks.
- Money base.
- M1.
- M3.
- Broad money.

The money categories of the Reserve Bank do not align with the five money classes identified above. However, there is a rough relationship that exists, and this is sufficient to calculate the size of each money class. Below is a summary of the relationship:

RBA category	Money class
Currency	Currency coins + Currency notes
Money base	Currency coins + Currency notes + Central bank money
Broad money	Currency coins + Currency notes + Central bank money + Commercial bank money

Each of the five money classes will now be examined.

KEEP READING

Chapter 8 :   Currency coins

Money plays the largest part in determining the course of history.

Karl Marx
The Communist Manifesto
1848

Money class

This is the first of five related chapters. The money class examined is that of currency coins, which are found in the pockets and piggy-banks of Australian residents.

Metal content

The public refer to the one and two dollar coins as gold coins. This is misleading since these coins do not contain gold, but rather they contain approximately:

- 92% copper
- 6% aluminium
- 2% nickel

Likewise, the coins referred to as silver coins contain approximately:

- 75% copper
- 25% nickel

Royal Australian Mint

The Royal Australian Mint states that its function is as follows:

> The Royal Australian Mint is a prescribed agency within the Commonwealth Government portfolio of the Treasury and is the **sole supplier of Australia's circulating coinage**.

The Mint is part of the Australian Treasury. It operates out of Canberra and manufactures two types of coins. They are:

- Circulating coins (i.e. 5, 10, 20, 50 cent coins plus $1 and $2 coins).
- Proof and uncirculating coins.

Circulating coins are legal tender, and used in the economy as a medium of exchange and to settle debts.

Selling to the RBA

The Annual Report of the Treasury for 2002 states that seigniorage is collected when coins are sold to the Reserve Bank of Australia:

> **1.23 Royal Australian Mint — seigniorage and repurchase of circulating coins**
>
> Seigniorage is collected by the Mint on behalf of the Commonwealth. Seigniorage represents the difference between the face value of coinage sold to the Reserve Bank of Australia and its cost of production to the Mint.

Proceeds from the sale of coins are remitted to the Commonwealth. In the Annual Report of the Royal Australian Mint for 2002 we find the following:

> The revenues from circulating coin sales are not directly available to be used by the Mint for its own purposes and are remitted to the Commonwealth's Official Public Account.

The Mint provides a list of amounts paid to the Commonwealth, with seigniorage heading the list at $129 million.

11 DETAILS OF PAYMENTS TO COMMONWEALTH

Seigniorage	129,538
Royalty on Numismatic Coin Sales	1,319
STOCP royalties prior years overpaid	(447)
Company and Payroll Tax Equivalents	924
Loss from Withdrawn Circulating Coin	(857)
Trust Fund Surplus paid to the Commonwealth	159
STOCP Royalty to Treasury	113
Capital injection	(313)
Seigniorage withheld	(2,990)
Actual Surplus Funds Paid to the Commonwealth	127,446

No further reporting

On 1 July 2005 the Royal Australian Mint became a prescribed agency within the Treasury portfolio. Consequently, the reporting structures at The Treasury and The Mint were altered. The Treasury no longer reports on the seigniorage received from The Mint. However, The Mint still provides the seigniorage numbers in their annual reports. For example, the following appears in the annual report of the Royal Australian Mint for 2016:

Finance Report

For the financial year 2015–16 the Mint reported a before tax operating surplus of $3.5 million and seigniorage payment of $88.5 million to the Commonwealth's Official Public Account.

Selling to commercial banks

In 2012 the Royal Australian Mint changed the way it distributes circulating coins. Previously it sold coins to the Reserve Bank of Australia. The 2016 annual report of the Royal Australian Mint states that they now sell coins directly to commercial banks. The relevant extract is below:

> Australian circulating coin finished good inventory is administered by the Mint on behalf of the Commonwealth. Two hundred and forty seven million pieces of administered inventory were sold to the commercial banks in 2015–16 with a face value of $140.8 million. Two hundred and fifty one million Australian circulating coins were produced, reflecting the increased demand from previous years.

Estimating seigniorage

The Royal Australian Mint does not provide a concise list of all seigniorage payments to the Australian Commonwealth. A proxy of the seigniorage is the revenue that the Royal Australian Mint receives from the sale of circulating coins. The table below is compiled from a number of annual reports of the Royal Australian Mint.

Year	Revenue (millions)
1965-75	$201.7
1975-85	$632.5
1985-95	$707.9
1995-05	$961.7
2006	$169.5
2007	$139.7
2008	$167.8
2009	$167.6
2010	$142.4
2011	$114.6
2012	$103.6
2013	$128.5
2014	$107.2
2015	$106.4
2016	$140.7

A portion of the table is reproduced below:

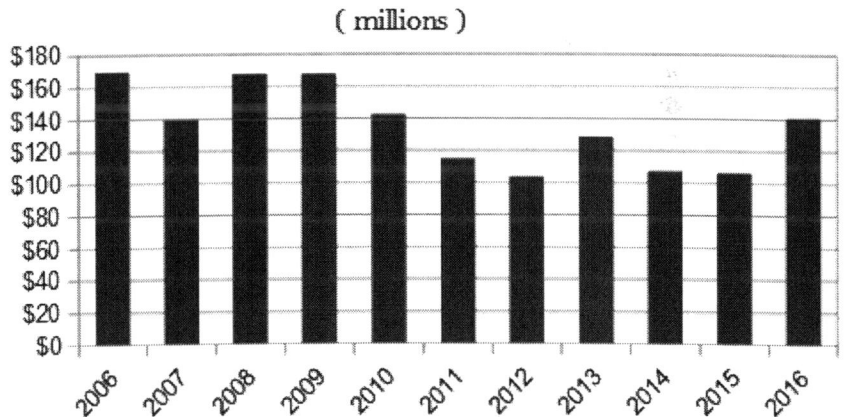

Revenue from sale of coins
(millions)

Coins & currency

An interesting statistic is the ratio between the value of coins and the value of coins and notes combined. To calculate the ratio, the following approach is used.

> Over the last 11 years, compare the increase in the value of coins (with figures from the Royal Australian Mint) against the increase in the value of coins and notes (with figures from the Reserve Bank).

From the Royal Australian Mint, we add up the revenue figures for the last 11 years and obtain $1,488 million. From the Reserve Bank we utilise their Monetary Aggregates spread sheet and note that the figure for currency (i.e. coins and notes) has grown by $34.186 billion over the same period.

	A	B
1	D3 MONETARY AGGREGATES	
2	Title	Currency
3	Frequency	Monthly
4	Units	$ billion
5	Source	RBA
6	Publication date	31-Oct-2016
557	Apr-2005	33.057
558	May-2005	32.858
559	Jun-2005	33.434
560	Jul-2005	33.817
561		
562	Apr-2016	66.778
563	May-2016	66.631
564	Jun-2016	67.620
565	Jul-2016	67.944
566	Aug-2016	67.809
567	Sep-2016	68.965
568	Oct-2016	

Increase of $34.186 billion in 11 years

Placing these figures into a ratio:

$$4.35\% = \frac{\$1,488 \text{ million (coins)}}{\$34,186 \text{ million (coins \& notes)}}$$

Coins constitute approximately 4.35% of the currency (i.e. coins and notes) in circulation.

Coins & broad money

Another statistic is the ratio between the value of coins and the value of all money in circulation. The amount of money in circulation is generally referred to as broad money. Wikipedia provides a simple definition:

> In economics, **broad money** is a measure of the money supply that includes more than just physical money such as currency and coins (also termed narrow money). It generally includes **demand deposits** at commercial banks, and any monies held in easily accessible accounts.

To calculate the ratio we use two figures from the RBA Monetary Aggregates spread sheet; the figure for broad money and the figure for currency. The figures are as at June 2016:

- Broad money = $1,893,505 million.
- Currency = $67,620 million (notes and coins).
- Coins relative to currency = 4.35% (as calculated above).

Placing these figures into a ratio we get:

$$0.16\% = \frac{4.35\% \ \times \ \$67,620 \text{ million (coins in use)}}{\$1,893,5050 \text{ million (broad money)}}$$

Coins constitute approximately 0.16% of the broad money supply.

Beneficiary

Between 1965 and 2016, the Royal Australian Mint received approximately $3.991 billion from the sale of circulating coins to the banking industry. The profit (i.e. the seigniorate) was paid to the Australian Commonwealth. This seigniorage has benefitted the people of Australia, since it was received in lieu of taxes.

Although the number is relatively small when compared to the $388 billion of federal tax receipts for the 2015-16 fiscal year; the principle highlighted above is very important - as will become apparent.

Chapter 9 :   Currency notes

Money is a new form of slavery, and distinguishable from the old simply by the fact that it is impersonal – that there is no human relation between master and slave.

Leo Tolstoy
Russian writer

Money class

The second money class examined is that of currency notes. Currency notes are included in the Reserve Bank measure of currency, money base and broad money.

Early bank notes

Prior to Australian Federation in 1901, commercial banks issued their own bank notes. On the following page is an image of a bank note issued by the Colonial Bank of Australasia in Melbourne. Printed across the face of the bank note are the words:

> The Colonial Bank of Australasia promise to pay to the bearer on demand at the office here ONE POUND Sterling.

During this period the term **one pound sterling** had a very specific meaning. Here a short history may suffice. Around 775, the Saxon kingdoms issued small silver coins called sterlings, and 240 of such sterlings were minted from a single pound of silver. With time and general use, the term **pound of sterlings** was shortened and became **pound sterling**.

Likewise, the term **note** is a shortening of the term **promissory note** or **bank promissory note**. Essentially, bank notes are promises or legal contracts whereby the holder is entitled to demand physical metal in exchange for the note. As shown on the note above; there is space for the manager and the accountant of the bank to sign the note – thereby rendering it a legal obligation.

Federation 1901

Prior to Federation in 1901, the currency circulating in Australia consisted of British copper, silver and gold coins, Australian gold coins, notes from private banks and notes from the Queensland State Government.

Although the Australian Constitution empowered Parliament to make laws regarding currency, coinage, legal tender and the issue of paper money, it wasn't until 1910 that the Australian Notes Act was passed. This act gave control of the issuance of Australian notes to the Commonwealth Treasury. The act made it an offence for banks to circulate notes that were issued by any of the states within Australia.

Similar to commercial bank notes, Australian notes also promised to pay the bearer on demand in precious metals. The first £10 note issued by the Commonwealth of Australia had the following on the face:

> The Treasurer of the Commonwealth of Australia promises to pay the bearer Ten Pounds in gold coin on demand at the Commonwealth Treasury at the seat of government.

An image of this note is below:

In 1910 the Bank Notes Act was passed. The act imposed a 10% tax on all bank notes issued by private banks – effectively discouraging but not prohibiting their general use.

In 1911 the Commonwealth Bank Act was passed, which established a commercial bank called the Commonwealth Bank of Australia. In 1920, the act was amended and control over the issuance of Australian notes was moved from the Commonwealth Treasury to the Australian Notes Board – which was an independent entity that operated within the Commonwealth Bank.

The relevant extract is shown below:

> " *Division* 4.—*Issue of Australian Notes.*
>
> " 60α.—(1.) Subject to this Act, the Board may from time to time—
>
> (a) issue Australian notes ;
> (b) re-issue Australian notes ; and
> (c) cancel Australian notes.
>
> " (2.) Australian notes issued in pursuance of this Part shall not be deemed to be bank notes within the meaning of the *Bank Notes Tax Act* 1910.

In 1924, the act was further amended and control over the issuance of Australian notes moved from the Australian Notes Board to the Board of Directors of the Commonwealth Bank. The act also empowered the Commonwealth Bank to issue Australian notes to other banks. The relevant extract is below:

> **18.** After section sixty o of the Principal Act the following section is inserted :—
>
> " 60oα. The Board may issue Australian notes to the Bank or to other banks in Australia in exchange for money or securities lodged with the London branch of the Bank.".

The effect of this last amendment was that other commercial banks could purchase Australian notes from the Commonwealth Bank, by lodging financial securities or money (i.e. gold and silver) at the London branch of the Commonwealth Bank. Banks wanting to enhance their standing readily took up this offer.

End of convertibility

The Commonwealth Bank Act of 1932 broke the link between newly issued Australian notes and precious metals. The act spanned all of two pages.

No. 16 of 1932.

An Act to amend the *Commonwealth Bank Act 1911-1931.*

[Assented to 21st May, 1932.]

B E it enacted by the King's Most Excellent Majesty, the Senate, and the House of Representatives of the Commonwealth of Australia, as follows :—

In terms of the act, holders of Australian notes were granted a period of grace within which to redeem their notes for precious metals. Holders of notes of one pound or less were given 20 years from the date of issue, while those with notes over one pound were given 40 years from the date of issue. The relevant section is below:

" (3.) For the purposes of the last preceding sub-section, notes of a denomination not exceeding One pound that have not been presented for payment within twenty years from the date of issue, and notes of a denomination exceeding One pound that have not been presented for payment within forty years from the date of issue, shall be deemed to have been redeemed and the amount of those notes shall be placed to the credit of a reserve account to which shall be debited the amount of any such notes subsequently presented and paid.

Shortly thereafter in 1933 a new series of Australian notes were issued. These notes no longer displayed a promise to pay the bearer gold or silver on demand. An example of an early £1 Australian note is below:

Note that on the face it says:

> One Pound legal tender in the Commonwealth and in all the territories under the control of the Commonwealth.

Current Australian notes have slightly different wording, namely:

> This Australian note is legal tender throughout Australia and its Territories.

Reserve Bank of Australia

In 1945 the Commonwealth Bank Act was passed. The act empowered the Commonwealth Bank to act as the sole issuer of Australian banknotes. In 1959 the Reserve Bank Act was passed, which resulted in the following:

- The Commonwealth Bank of Australia was renamed the Reserve Bank of Australia. This entity currently acts as the central bank in Australia.
- All commercial banking functions of the Reserve Bank of Australia were transferred into a new body corporate. This new entity assumed the old name, namely the Commonwealth Bank of Australia.

The act took effect on 14 January 1960. The result is that the Reserve Bank now issues all Australian notes. The manufacture of the notes is done by Note Printing Australia, which is a wholly owned subsidiary of the Reserve Bank.

Distribution of profits

Before examining the seigniorage that flows from the production and sale of currency notes, it is instructive to examine how the profits of the Reserve Bank are distributed. Section 30 of the Reserve Bank Act of 1959 states that the profits of the bank must be managed as follows:

(a) such amount as the Treasurer, after consultation with the Reserve Bank Board, determines is to be set aside for **contingencies**; and

(b) such amount as the Treasurer, after consultation with the Reserve Bank Board, determines shall be placed to the credit of the Reserve Bank Reserve Fund; and

(c) the remainder shall be **paid to the Commonwealth**.

The Reserve Bank does not make a profit each and every year. A graphic from the Reserve Bank conveys this fact:

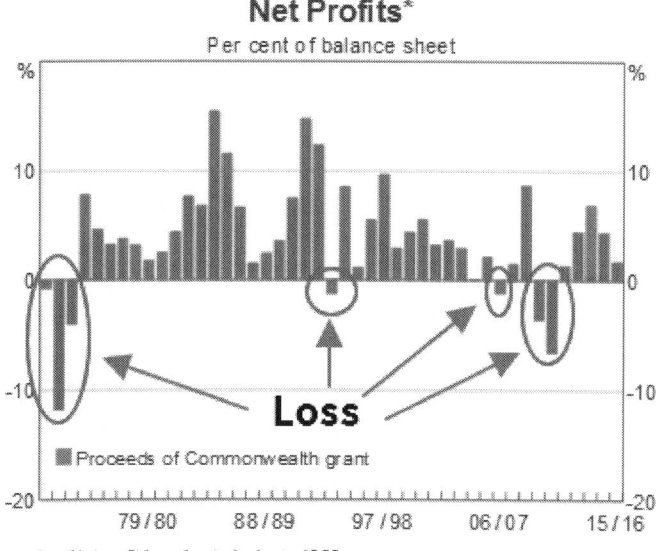

Net Profits*
Per cent of balance sheet

Loss

■ Proceeds of Commonwealth grant

79/80   88/89   97/98   06/07   15/16

*   Net profit is estimated prior to 1998
Source: RBA

Central bank seigniorage

The Reserve Bank does not apply the general definition of seigniorage to its manufacture and sale of Australian notes. The general definition states that if the cost to manufacture a $100 note is negligible, then the seigniorage on the sale of the note is $100.

The Reserve Bank applies a different approach. Below is an extract from a communiqué with the Reserve Bank:

> With the money the Reserve Bank of Australia receives when banknotes are sold to banks, the Reserve Bank buys government securities that generate an interest income... Consequently, **seigniorage is measured as the difference between the interest income from government securities and the cost of banknote production.**

In a nutshell; the approach of the Reserve Bank is that seigniorage is the profit that flows from various investments, where the investments were made using the revenue from the sale of the currency notes.

Accrual approach

From an accounting perspective; the general definition of seigniorage fits into the **cash flow** approach, while the seigniorage used by the Reserve Bank fits into the **accrual** approach. The Reserve Bank Bulletin of July 1997 states the following:

> Over long periods the two approaches should yield similar estimates of seigniorage ...

To test this statement, a comparison is performed. The seigniorage using the cash flow approach is $100. The seigniorage using the accrual approach is calculated by adding the present value of all income generated from a financial security purchased for $100. The following assumptions are used:

- The Reserve Bank buys a bond for $100.
- The bond has a long duration (i.e. 100 years).
- The bond pays interest of 5%.
- The interest payments are discounted at 5%.

The figures are placed into a spread sheet and the present values are calculated. The first five rows are below:

Year	Income	Present value	Running total
1	$5	$4.76	$4.76
2	$5	$4.54	$9.30
3	$5	$4.32	$13.62
4	$5	$4.11	$17.73
5	$5	$3.92	$21.65

The last three rows in the spread sheet are below:

Year	Income	Present value	Running total
98	$5	$0.04	$99.16
99	$5	$0.04	$99.20
100	$5	$0.04	$99.24
		$99.24	

The total of all the present values is $99.24. Consequently, the statement by the Reserve Bank is accurate. However, the practical effect is that the financial benefits are spread into the future – thereby delaying the benefit to the Commonwealth.

Buy with central bank money

When commercial banks buy currency notes from the Reserve Bank, they pay with central bank money. Below is an extract from the Reserve Bank web site:

> When Authorised Deposit-taking Institutions [i.e. commercial banks] purchase banknotes from the Reserve Bank, settlement is in **Exchange Settlement funds** [i.e. central bank money].

Central bank money can only exist by being borrowed from the Reserve Bank. This topic is discussed in detail in a subsequent chapter.

Notes & broad money

An interesting statistic is the ratio between the value notes and the value of all money in circulation. For this calculation we adapt the figures in a previous chapter:

- Broad money = $1,893,505 million.
- Currency = $67,620 million (notes and coins).
- Notes relative to currency = 95.65% (calculated in Chapter 8).

Placing the figures into a ratio we get:

$$3.42\% = \frac{95.65\% \times \$67,620 \text{ million (notes in use)}}{\$1,893,505 \text{ million (broad money)}}$$

Notes constitute approximately 3.42% of the broad money supply.

Sale of bank notes

The Reserve Bank Annual Report 2016 provides a graphic of the value of currency notes purchased by the commercial banks. During the global financial crisis of 2008, the demand for currency notes increased dramatically.

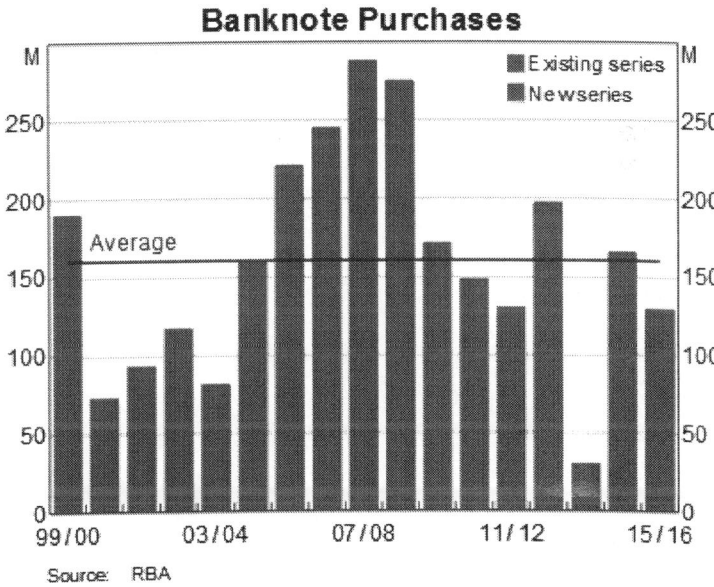

Beneficiary

As at June 2016, the Reserve Bank had issued $70.2 billion of currency notes into circulation. The figures used to generate the graph below were obtained from the Reserve Bank spread sheet entitled Banknotes on Issue by Denomination.

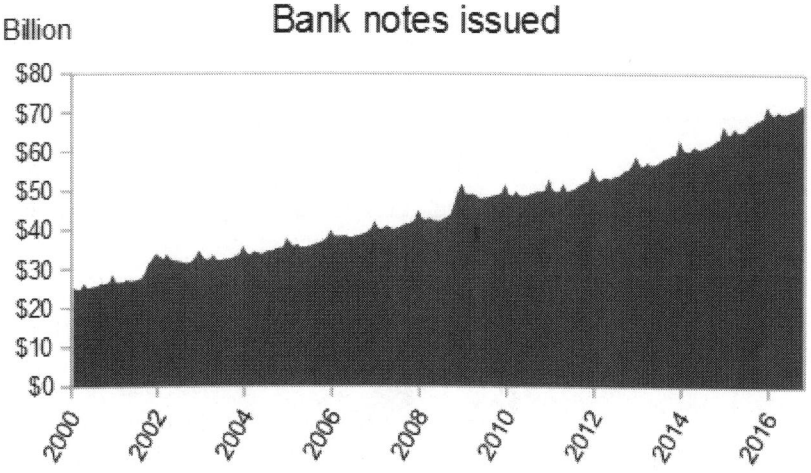

If the Reserve Bank applied the cash flow approach to seigniorage, then $70.2 billion would have flowed to the Commonwealth at the time of sale.

Now or later

Since the Reserve Bank applies the accrual approach to seigniorage, the financial benefits that flow to the Commonwealth are delayed.

It is easy to speculate that the average Australian would prefer to receive a financial benefit immediately (possibly in the form of reduced taxes), rather than a series of smaller benefits extending over their life and the lives of their children.

Chapter 10 :   Gold and silver coins

When a government is dependent upon bankers for money, they and not the leaders of the government control the situation, since the hand that gives is above the hand that takes... Money has no motherland; financiers are without patriotism and without decency; their sole object is gain.

Napoleon Bonaparte
Emperor of France
1815

Money class

The third money class examined is that of gold and silver coins (comprised of precious metals). There are two bodies in Australia authorised to manufacture these uncirculating coins, namely the Royal Australian Mint and the Perth Mint.

Creators

The Royal Australian Mint is an Australian Government agency prescribed under the Financial Management and Accountability Act of 1997. The Gold Corporation (of which the Perth Mint is a subsidiary) is owned by the Government of Western Australia. The Perth Mint produces uncirculating coins under agreement with the Australian Government.

Legal tender

Uncirculating coins, which bear the image of Her Majesty Queen Elizabeth II on the front of the coin, are considered to be legal tender. The Currency Act of 1965 defines both coins and legal tender. The relevant extracts are:

Section 14(A) defines coins:

> Coins of a denomination of $5 or more; or whose standard composition consists of, or includes, gold, silver or platinum;

Section 22(2) defines legal tender:

> A tender of payment of money is a legal tender if it is made in coins that are made and issued under this Act and are of current weight:

The Perth Mint Annual Report 2008 confirms that the precious metal coins that they produce are legal tender.

BULLION COINS AND BARS

- Gold Corporation, the operator of The Perth Mint, is the producer of Australia's official investment or bullion coins.
- Each coin is issued as legal tender under the *Australian Currency Act 1965*.

Beneficiary

The Perth Mint pays seigniorage to the Australian Government on the sale of uncirculating coins. In their Annual Report 2016 they state:

> Seigniorage royalty payments to the Australian Federal Treasury, relating to the terms of the agreement under which Gold Corporation mints and issues Australian legal tender coins, was $4.37 million for the year.

The Perth Mint also pays taxes and dividends to the government of Western Australia. The same annual report states:

> Payments to the Government of Western Australia during the financial year included income tax equivalent payments totalling $5.07 million and a dividend of $10.54 million.

The annual report states that over the last 10 years, the Perth Mint has paid a total of $200 million to the government of Western Australian.

Summary

The Perth Mint and the Royal Australian Mint contribute to the coffers of both state and federal governments, be it in the form of taxes, dividends or seigniorage. The common denominator is that both organisations operate for the benefit of Australia. The financial benefits that flow from the creation of money are passed onto the residents of Australia.

This simple principle is at the core of the Fair Money solution.

KEEP READING

Chapter 11 : Commercial bank money

I am afraid the ordinary citizen will not like to be told that the banks can and do create money. And they who control the credit of the nation direct the policy of Governments and hold in the hollow of their hand the destiny of the people.

Reginald McKenna
Chairman of the Midland Bank
Addressing stockholders in 1924.

Money class

The fourth money class examined is that of commercial bank money. Commercial bank money constitutes the largest class of money in Australia. All commercial bank money is in electronic form and can only exist within the confines of the commercial banking network.

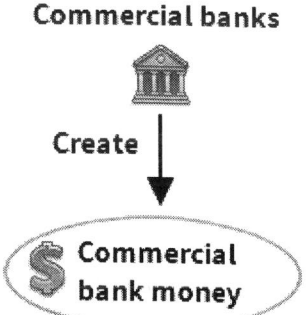

Debt monetisation

Commercial bank money is created via debt monetisation. When banks create commercial bank money, they record the new money (i.e. the deposit) as a liability in their balance sheet, while they simultaneously record the debt obligation of the client as an asset in their balance sheet.

By way of example: if Mr Jones applies for a loan of $500,000 and the bank agrees to lend the money; then after the legal agreements are signed the bank posts a journal entry that affects their balance sheet as follows:

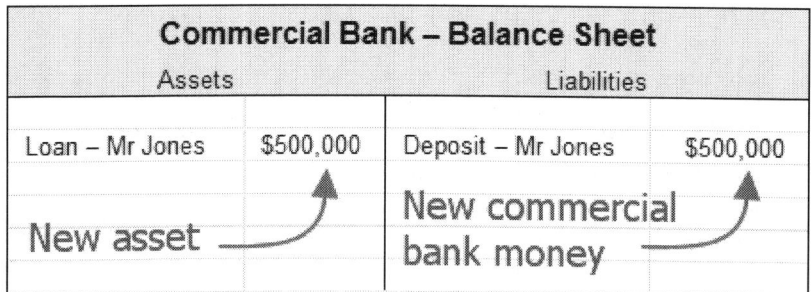

The deposit of $500,000 can be transferred to a different account at the same bank, or to an account at a different bank. Commercial bank money always appears as a liability in bank balance sheets.

 They simultaneously create a loan and a deposit without having to take the money out of the account of any other savers.

> Professor Steve Keen
> University of Western Sydney
> Interviewed by Chris Martenson on 8 June 2012

The quote above accentuates the fact that when banks make loans (i.e. when they monetise debt), they do not touch the deposits of other banking clients.

Growth of 9.7%

To estimate the quantity of commercial bank money in circulation we reference the Monetary Aggregates spread sheet from the Reserve Bank of Australia, and apply the following formula:

$$\text{Commercial bank money} = \text{Broad money} - \text{Money base}$$

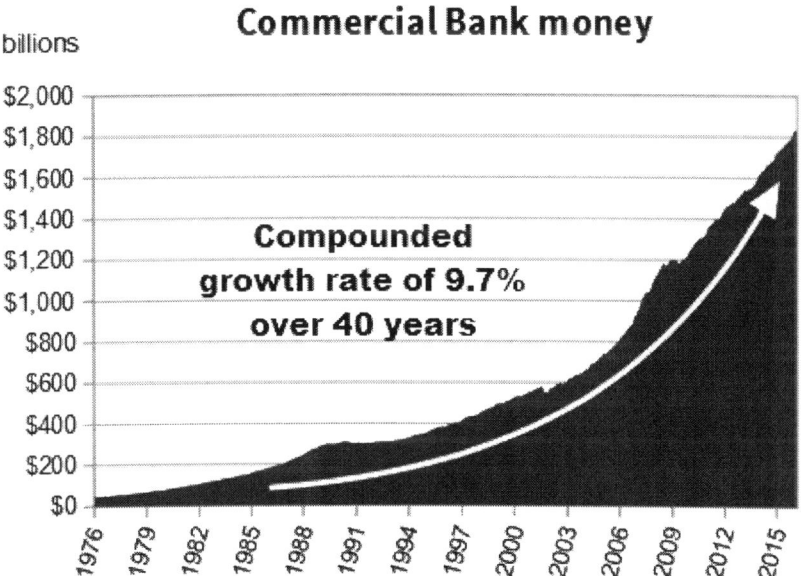

Commercial bank money increased from a paltry $45 billion in August 1976 to a staggering $1,827 billion in August 2016. This is an annual compounded growth rate of 9.76% over 40 years - a number well in excess of the Australian population growth rate or the GDP growth rate.

No seigniorage

Commercial banks do not report on any seigniorage that flows from the creation of commercial bank money. As a simple test; the Annual Report of the Commonwealth Bank of Australia for 2015 does not use the word seigniorage anywhere in the document.

The reason is that commercial banks maintain the position that they act as intermediaries between lenders and borrowers (which is false). Should the word seigniorage be mentioned, those with a modicum of intellect would start questioning the publically stated role of commercial banks.

Opportunity cost

Investopedia defines opportunity cost as follows:

> The cost of an alternative that must be forgone in order to pursue a certain action. Put another way, **the benefits you could have received by taking an alternative action**.

If the government created and spent into circulation all the digital money used within the economy, then the financial benefit thereof would accrue to the public. Since this does not occur, there is a real and measureable opportunity cost borne by the public.

 The Government should create, issue, and circulate all the currency and credits needed to satisfy the spending power of the Government and the buying power of consumers. By the adoption of these principles, **the taxpayers will be saved immense sums of interest**. Money will cease to be master and become the servant of humanity.

Abraham Lincoln

As at September 2016, the opportunity cost of commercial banks creating commercial bank money stood at approximately **$1.831 trillion**. With each passing year this figure increases by approximately $100 billion.

Australian Federal Government expenditure for 2016 was $425 billion. If the government created and spent $100 billion into circulation, this would have resulted in a 23% reduction of funds required for government expenditure. Imagine the public elation if taxes were reduced by this percentage - while keeping government expenditure at the same level.

Chapter 12 : Central bank money

The bank hath benefit of interest on all moneys which it creates out of nothing.

William Paterson
Founder of the Bank of England

Money class

The fifth money class examined is that of central bank money, which is created by the Reserve Bank of Australia.

Money held in deposit accounts at the Reserve Bank can only move between such accounts and do not find their way into the economy. Central bank money is included in the Reserve Bank measure of base money.

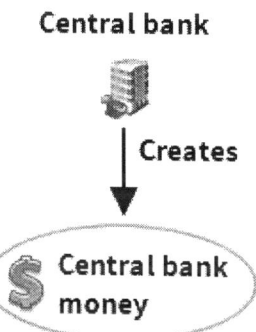

Central bank

Creates

Central bank money

Deposit accounts

There are two types of accounts at the Reserve Bank into which central bank money is deposited. They are:

- Exchange Settlement accounts.
- General Deposit accounts.

The Reserve Bank provides a definition of Exchange Settlement accounts:

> An account held at the Reserve Bank of Australia by financial institutions to settle financial obligations arising from the clearing of payments.

The Reserve Bank Liabilities and Assets spread sheet identifies the holders of the General Deposit accounts:

Deposits (excluding Exchange Settlement balances) include deposits of the Bank's customers, namely the Australian Government, overseas institutions, including the IMF and central banks, and state governments and authorities.

In a nutshell; General Deposit accounts are used predominantly by non-commercial banks, while Exchange Settlement accounts are used predominantly by commercial banks. Exchange Settlement accounts are used to facilitate inter-bank payments, and how they function is detailed in a subsequent chapter.

Account balances

The Reserve Bank Liabilities and Assets Summary spread sheet lists the amount of central bank money deposited into Exchange Settlement accounts and General Deposit accounts. The totals are displayed below. These balances do not increase gradually on an annual basis; they fluctuate in response to economic events and regulatory requirements.

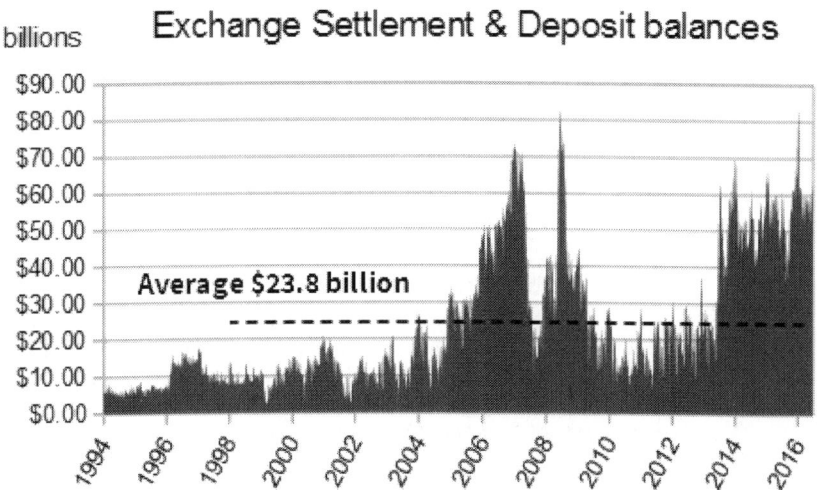

The average amount of deposits in the diagram above is $23.8 billion. Note #9 in the Reserve Bank Annual Report of 2016 identifies the largest holders of central bank money to be:

- The Australian Government and
- The financial institutions that maintain Exchange Settlement accounts.

Note 9 – Deposits

	2015 $M
Exchange Settlement balances	23,360
Australian Government	36,294
State governments	59
Foreign governments, foreign institutions and international organisations	758
Other depositors	15
As at 30 June	60,486

Reserve accounts

The public is familiar with the term reserve account, and has the notion that it refers to an account that a commercial bank holds at the central bank. This terminology is correct within the context of the United States; where commercial banks hold reserve accounts at the Federal Reserve System.

The terminology is different in Australia; as reserve accounts are called Exchange Settlement accounts, and the accounts are held at the Reserve Bank of Australia. Since this book has an Australian bias, the local vernacular is retained.

Exchange Settlement accounts

The Reserve Bank published an article in March 1999 entitled The Role of Exchange Settlement Accounts. Although dated, it does provide a good overview of how these accounts operate. Below is an extract:

> The banks have merely used **central bank-issued money** to **settle the obligations** between themselves.

The extract is explicit in stating that central bank money is used for inter-bank payments. The Reserve Bank provides details on their web site regarding the processes whereby commercial banks obtain central bank money:

> Counterparties are able to sell highly rated **debt securities** to the Reserve Bank either under repurchase agreement (repo) or outright sale. Under a repo, the seller agrees to repurchase the security at a future time and at a pre-agreed price. In many respects, **the transaction is similar to a secured loan**, with the difference between the purchase and repurchase prices representing the interest earned on the transaction.

The extract can be summarised as follows:

- The central bank lends central bank money against debt securities.
- These transactions are similar to secured loans.

Described above is similar to commercial banks when they lend money to clients, i.e. when they monetise debt. Commercial banks record the loan obligation of their clients as an asset, while the Reserve Bank records the financial instrument as an asset. The Reserve Bank Annual Report of 2015 shows the largest asset on their balance sheet to be **Australian dollar investments**:

	Note	2015 $M
Assets		
Cash and cash equivalents	6	438
Australian dollar investments	1(b), 15	86,294
Foreign exchange	1(b), 15	65,241
Gold	1(c), 15	3,915
Property, plant and equipment	1(d), 8, 16	549
Loans, advances and other assets	7	476
Total Assets		156,913

Note #1(b) provides details of the Australian dollar investments:

> The RBA holds Australian Government Securities and securities issued by the central borrowing authorities of state and territory governments. These holdings include fixed coupon, inflation

indexed and discount securities. It also holds under **reverse repurchase agreements**: bank bills, certificates of deposit and **debt securities** of authorised deposit-taking institutions licensed in Australia.

The common thread in the list of financial instruments above is that each is a **debt security**, with most used to facilitate repurchase agreements.

Repurchase agreements

Repurchase agreements are the largest sub-category of Australian dollar investments. The Reserve Bank provides the following analysis:

Maturity Analysis – as at 30 June 2015

	Balance sheet total $M	Contracted maturity $M				
		On demand	0 to 3 months	3 to 12 months	1 to 5 years	Over 5 years
Assets						
Cash and cash equivalents	438	32	405	...	...	
Australian dollar investments						
Securities sold under repurchase agreements	–	...	–	...	...	...
Securities purchased under repurchase agreements	76,183	–	52,800	1,969	...	...
Other securities	9,930	...	1,404	6,318	899	1,309
Accrued interest	181	–	137	44	...	–
	86,294					

The Reserve Bank defines a repurchase agreement as follows:

> Under a repo, the seller agrees to repurchase the security at a future time and at a pre-agreed price.

By way of example: A commercial bank enters into a repurchase agreement with the Reserve Bank. The first part of the agreement is the sale of a government bond to the Reserve Bank for $1 million. The Reserve Bank monetises the bond and deposits $1 million into the Exchange Settlement account of the commercial bank. The Reserve Bank records the bond as an asset and the deposit as a liability.

Just as banks can create money, the commercial banks can create money by double entry book keeping. So can **central banks**...

Professor Steve Keen
University of Western Sydney
Interviewed by Chris Martenson on 8 June 2012

Average term

The diagram below shows that the average term of repurchase agreements to be approximately 21 days.

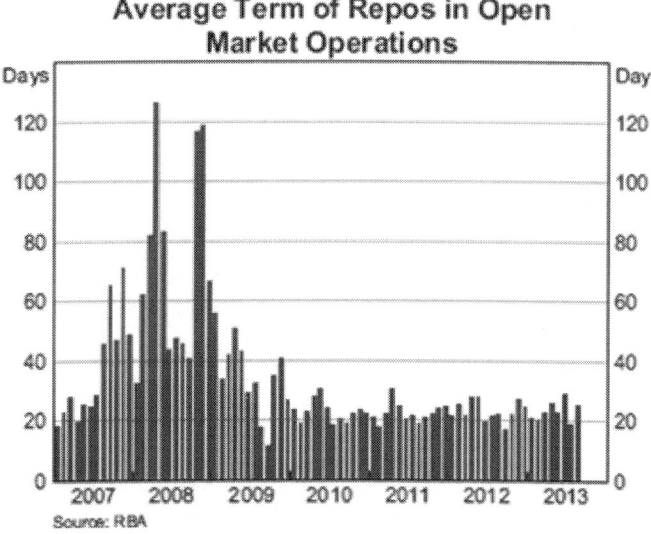

The second part of the agreement is when the commercial bank buys the bond back from the Reserve Bank. Normally the repurchase price will be higher than the original sale price. Assume that after 21 days the commercial bank pays $1,004,000 for the return of the bond. The difference of $4,000 is the interest that the commercial bank pays to the Reserve Bank for the use of $1 million.

Repetition

Repurchase agreements are executed on a regular basis and follow the pattern below:

- The central bank monetises a debt security and creates new money.
- After a short period, the central bank demonetises the debt security and destroys existing central bank money.
- The average duration of a repurchase agreement is 21 days.

Below is the balance sheet of the Reserve Bank when it records the first part of the repurchase agreement. When the second part is implemented, the Reserve Bank reverses the transaction and records the interest earned.

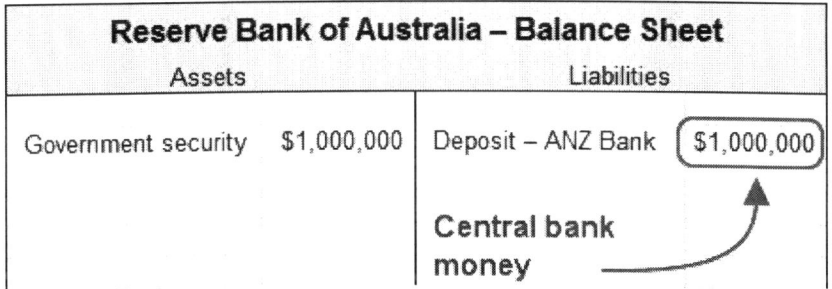

Reserve Bank of Australia – Balance Sheet	
Assets	Liabilities
Government security $1,000,000	Deposit – ANZ Bank $1,000,000
	Central bank money

Commercial banks use central bank money to purchase currency notes and to make inter-bank payments.

Seigniorage

Seigniorage is the difference between the face value of money and the cost to produce such money (be it physical currency or digital deposits). The Reserve Bank does not record seigniorage when it creates central bank money (i.e. digital money). This situation is similar to commercial banks when they create commercial bank money.

Consequently, seigniorage on central bank money is effectively forgone.

Opportunity cost

There is a measurable opportunity cost (i.e. a loss of potential financial benefit) borne by the Australian public as a result of the Reserve Bank not recording seigniorage on central bank money.

As at 30 June 2015 the amount of central bank money in deposit accounts stood at **$60.48 billion.** This is the amount of seigniorage foregone.

Liabilities

Deposits	1(b), 9	60,486
Distribution payable to the Commonwealth	1(g), 3	2,501
Australian notes on issue	1(b), 15	65,481
Other liabilities	10	4,576
Total Liabilities		133,044

Chapter 13 : Fractional reserve banking

The banks do create money. They have been doing it for a long time ... and they did not admit it.

H. W. White
Chairman of the Associated Banks of New Zealand
New Zealand Monetary Commission (1955)

Straw man

Many well intentioned people campaign for a just monetary system on the basis that our **current monetary system** is based on a fractional reserve banking model. This is a straw man, which Wikipedia defines as follows:

A straw man is a common form of argument and is an informal fallacy based on giving the impression of refuting an opponent's argument, while actually refuting an argument which was not advanced by that opponent.

The term fractional reserve banking is often used with reckless abandon, as if the mere use thereof is proof that the orator has a grasp on the subject. Empirically, it takes but a few pointed questions to render their argument impotent. Those in academia understand well enough that a sound thesis cannot be based on flawed assumptions. Yet, reference to this defective thesis continues to be employed. For resolution, we turn to the root of this metastasized idea.

Two models

Examining explanations of how fractional reserve banking works, quickly leads to a state of confusion. The reason is simple; there are two distinct models of fractional reserve banking, with each purporting to explain our current monetary system. Since the models are different, we can already conclude that one must be flawed. As demonstrated below – both models are in fact flawed. These two models are:

- Deposit model (a repetitive process)
- Multiplier model (a single process)

The Deposit model outlines a repetitive process whereby a commercial bank receives a deposit, withholds a portion of the deposit (calling it a reserve) and then lending the balance.

The Multiplier model provides a formula that is applied by a commercial bank to determine the amount of money that it can create. Both of these models are straw men.

Genesis

In May 1961, the Federal Reserve Bank of Chicago published a booklet entitled Modern Money Mechanics. The booklet explains the mechanism of money creation in the United States, and has become a seminal source to numerous articles that purport to explain fractional reserve banking.

Before examining the contents of the booklet, it is useful to examine the most common explanations of the Deposit model and the Multiplier model. What is proffered below differs only marginally from that found on financial web sites, YouTube or in academic textbooks.

Deposit model

The Deposit model presented is the one most commonly promoted. RationalWiki offers the following definition of fractional reserve banking:

> Fractional-reserve banking refers to a banking system where the bank holds a fraction of the demand deposits it receives, and loans out the rest. It is the primary mode of operation of nearly all retail banks in the modern world.

To create an example of the Deposit model requires two assumptions; i.e. a client deposits $1,000 and the reserve rate is 10%. The Deposit model proceeds along the following lines:

- The client deposits $1,000.
- The bank retains $100 for reserves (i.e. 10%).
- The bank lends $900 to a new borrower.
- The borrower deposits $900.
- The bank retains $90 for reserves (i.e. 10%).
- The bank lends $810 to a new borrower.
- And so on…

With the assistance of a spread sheet, we calculate the resulting figures. Using the round function to calculate the reserve amount, the first five iterations look as follows:

#	Deposit	Reserve (10%)	Lend out	Total lending
1	$1,000.00	$100.00	$900.00	$900.00
2	$900.00	$90.00	$810.00	$1,710.00
3	$810.00	$81.00	$729.00	$2,439.00
4	$729.00	$72.90	$656.10	$3,095.10
5	$656.10	$65.61	$590.49	$3,685.59

Traversing down the spread sheet, the 93rd iteration is the last row where a single cent can be set aside as a reserve. Beyond that point the spread sheet generates a zero value for the reserve amount.

#	Deposit	Reserve (10%)	Lend out	Total lending
89	$0.09	$0.01	$0.08	$8,998.68
90	$0.08	$0.01	$0.07	$8,998.75
91	$0.07	$0.01	$0.06	$8,998.81
92	$0.06	$0.01	$0.05	$8,998.86
93	$0.05	$0.01	$0.04	$8,998.90
	$9,998.86			

Sum of all deposits

After adding the deposit amounts in the first column (and rounding the total), we can draw the following conclusion:

> Applying the Deposit model (with a reserve rate of 10%) allows a bank to take an initial deposit of $1,000 and to make a series of loans – culminating in the total deposits at the bank being $10,000.

If the reserve rate is altered, the model dictates that the total amount of money that the bank can lend varies. The table below lists some of the permutations.

Initial Deposit	Reserve rate	Bank can lend	Total Deposits
$1,000	0%	unlimited	unlimited
$1,000	1%	$99,000	$100,000
$1,000	5%	$19,000	$20,000
$1,000	10%	$9,000	$10,000
$1,000	20%	$4,000	$5,000
$1,000	50%	$1,000	$2,000
$1,000	80%	$250	$1,250
$1,000	100%	$0	$1,000

Repudiation

The Deposit model relies on the assumption that commercial banks withhold a portion of any deposit, and lend the balance. Had the authors of the Deposit model read the entire booklet Modern Money Mechanics, they would have found the following on page 6:

Of course, they do not really pay out loans from the money they receive as deposits. If they did this, no additional money would be created. What they do when they make loans is to accept promissory notes in exchange for credits to the borrowers' transaction accounts. Loans (assets) and deposits (liabilities) both rise by $9,000.

This simple repudiation by the Federal Reserve is sufficient to relegate the Deposit model to the dustbin of history. Its longevity can only be ascribed to selective reading. Of interest is the fact that the latter half of the extract describes the process of debt monetisation.

Multiplier model

The Multiplier model is more practical than the Deposit model. It recognises two money classes, and is simple to implement. Wikipedia provides the following definition:

Most often, it [the money multiplier] measures the maximum amount of commercial bank money that can be created by a given unit of central bank money

The formula used in the Multiplier model looks as follows:

$$\text{Max commercial bank money} = \frac{\text{Reserves (central bank money)}}{\text{Reserve rate}}$$

$$\$10,000 = \frac{\$1,000}{10\%}$$

The model states that if a commercial bank holds $1,000 of central bank money and if the reserve rate is 10%, then the bank is entitled to create $10,000 of commercial bank money. The process described in the Multiplier model is different to that of the Deposit model. Despite this difference, people continue to offer up both models when attempting to explain how our modern banking system works.

Repudiation

Page 37 of the Modern Money Mechanics booklet addresses the Multiplier model as follows:

> **In the real world, a bank's lending is not normally constrained by the amount of excess reserves it has at any given moment.** Rather, loans are made, or not made, depending on the bank's credit policies and its expectations about its ability to obtain the funds necessary to pay its customers' checks and maintain required reserves in a timely fashion.

This means that the amount of central bank money that a commercial bank holds, does not influence the bank when it creates commercial bank money (i.e. when it monetises a debt). This extract from the Federal Reserve renders the Multiplier model meaningless.

In May 2010 two staff members at the Federal Reserve Board Washington D.C. authored an article entitled Money, Reserves, and the Transmission of Monetary Policy: Does the Money Multiplier Exist? An extract is provided below:

> Simple textbook treatments of the money multiplier give the quantity of bank reserves a causal role in determining the quantity of money... Using data from recent decades, we have demonstrated that **this simple textbook link is implausible** in the United States.

This extract confirms that reserves do not limit banks in their creation of commercial bank money. The Multiplier model should also be consigned to the dustbin of history.

Reserve Bank of Australia

In the United States, commercial banks have reserve accounts which are held at the Federal Reserve System. In Australia, commercial banks have Exchange Settlement accounts which are held at the Reserve Bank of Australia.

In the Reserve Bank Annual Report for 2014, we find an explanation on the use of Exchange Settlement accounts:

> While required local currency-denominated central bank reserves are used as an instrument for monetary policy in other countries, **their purpose in Australia is purely to meet liquidity requirements for the smooth functioning of the payments system.**

These accounts are used for inter-bank payments. They do not constrain commercial banks when they lend money.

The Multiplier model states that the level of reserves determines the amount of money created. The Federal Reserve and the Reserve Bank of Australia have both repudiated this causal relationship.

Deposits affect reserves

Bank reserves (or central bank deposits) do not constrain commercial banks when they create commercial bank money. However, there is a reverse relationship that exists. The following quotes are offered:

In the real world, banks extend credit, creating deposits in the process, and look for the reserves later.

Alan Holmes
Senior Vice President (1969)
Federal Reserve Bank of New York

 After the banks have created new money, then the reserve they need to match the new money they have created are determined.

Professor Steve Keen
University of Western Sydney
Interviewed by Chris Martenson on 8 June 2012

A graphic of the relationship between commercial bank money and central bank reserves is provided below:

Central bank

Exchange Settlement Account	Amount
Commercial bank	$100

Deposits affect reserves

Commercial bank

Deposit Accounts	Amount
Mr Green	$1,000
Mr Jones	$550
Mrs Blue	$2,500

Goldsmiths

The Deposit model and the Multiplier model have no relevance in our current banking system. This does not diminish the fact that fractional reserve banking was practiced in decades past.

Returning to the booklet Modern Money Mechanics, we repeat the section that deals with the creation of money when gold and silver was a medium of exchange:

> **It started with goldsmiths.** As early bankers, they initially provided safekeeping services, making a profit from vault storage fees for gold and coins deposited with them. ... Then, bankers discovered that they could make loans merely by giving their promises to pay, or bank notes, to borrowers. In this way, **banks began to create money. More notes could be issued than the gold and coin on hand** because only a portion of the notes outstanding would be presented for payment at any one time.

The last sentence in the extract above is the essence of fractional reserve banking.

Protracted demise

In Australia, fractional reserve banking commenced a slow demise with the passing of the Commonwealth Bank Act of 1932.

The act provided a period of grace to Australian note holders, where they had 20 years from the date of issue to redeem notes of one pound or less, and 40 years from the date of issue to redeem notes greater than a pound. From 1933 all newly issued Australian notes were fiat.

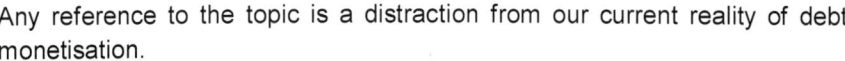

Today, fractional reserve banking is not practiced by any commercial bank in any shape or form. Any reference to the topic is a distraction from our current reality of debt monetisation.

Chapter 14 : Bank obfuscation

Each and every time a bank makes a loan; new bank credit is created – new deposits – brand new money.

Graham Towers
Former governor of the Central Bank of Canada
1939

Misdirection

The National Australia Bank published a page on its web site with the heading: **How banks work**. For any student researching this topic, one would assume that there could be no greater authority on the subject than a major commercial bank.

The National Australia Bank (NAB) posed a hypothetical question; where do banks get their money from? They then proceeded to answer the question. Visitors to the site had the ability to post comments or questions.

The answer from the NAB (reproduced on the following page) follows the mantra of "Banks get their money from depositors", and they stay clear of the fact that commercial banks monetise debt and that the deposits of existing clients are unaffected when making loans.

 When banks extend loans to their customers, they create money by crediting their customers' accounts.

Sir Mervyn King
Governor of the Bank of England
2003-2013

Source of funds

What follows is comical were it not so shameful in its blatant obfuscation. Below is the answer of the National Australia Bank to its hypothetical question. From the answer they would have us believe that there are two sources of money when commercial banks make loans, namely:

- Deposits at their own bank.
- Deposits at other banks (obtained via the inter-bank market).

We examine each source in turn. Regarding the use of deposits at their own bank; the Bank of England, the International Monetary Fund and the Federal Reserve Bank of New York have stated unambiguously that commercial banks create money when loans are made, and that existing deposits are left unaffected.

How banks work

16 November 2010

Where do banks get their money from?

Banks get most of their money from deposits. They keep a certain percentage of this sum aside in case people want their money and lend out the rest. They can also borrow money in the interbank lending market from other banks for which they are charged interest just like us.

When the National Australia Bank states that banks keep a certain percentage of deposits aside, they are promoting the Deposit model. This theoretical model has been soundly repudiated by the Federal Reserve System.

Regarding the use of deposits at other banks; when commercial banks borrow money from other banks in the inter-bank market, they only borrow central bank money, and not commercial bank money. As the Reserve Bank of Australia has pointed out, central bank money does not flow into the economy, but only moves between accounts maintained at the central bank level.

Listing depositors

Members of the public are allowed to post comments on the National Australia Bank web page. A person by the name of Bill raised the following question: "Where does the bank get money to lend for mortgages?" The response from the National Australia Bank is provided below, and deserves some investigation.

NAB *says:*

May 18, 2012 at 4:48 pm

Hi Bill, around 65% of our funding for lending comes from money deposited with NAB by our customers. 35% of our funds are sourced from the global wholesale market from large institutional investors such as superannuation and investment funds and international banks. Around 1/3 of this comes from domestic investors and 2/3 from overseas investors.

What the National Australia Bank has done is list their depositors by category. Underlined is the largest category, namely ordinary members of the public and the corporations that operate in Australia.

The obvious question that should be asked is this; has any member of the public or any corporation in Australia ever looked at their bank statement and noticed that their deposits are missing – supposedly having been lent out as mortgage financing?

The answer to this question is an emphatic and unqualified no. No person or corporation has ever examined their bank statement to find their deposits missing due to bank lending. If this ever occurred, there would be riots in the streets and depositors would be at their local bank branches demanding an explanation or intent on withdrawing their deposits.

Rather than banks receiving deposits when households save and then lending them out, bank lending creates deposits.

Money creation in the modern economy
The Bank of England
2014

It is disheartening to observe a major commercial bank responding to a simple question in this manner. One can only hope that such public pronouncements are done in ignorance and not with the full knowledge of how our monetary system actually works.

Perception

Members of the public are acutely aware that something is amiss with our current monetary system. Instead of commercial banks being a source of accurate information, the perception is that commercial banks are deliberately contributing to the confusion that exists within the general public.

Terms such as debt monetization, creation of money and seigniorage are eschewed by the financial industry and the media alike. Yet, these terms and concepts are the bedrock of our current monetary system.

Industries have to evolve in order to stay relevant and to survive. An informed public and the correct use of terminology is the first step in a healthy debate on the subject of money creation and its role in the service of mankind.

Chapter 15 :   Depositors are creditors

The money deposited in an account is no longer deemed as belonging to the principal but rather to the bank. In this relationship the bank is only contractually accountable for the sum of the money paid in.

Dalvinder Singh
Banking Regulation of UK and US Financial Markets
2007

Deposits

When you park your car in a public garage, it remains your property. Your car does not become the property of the owners of the garage, and your car

will never appear on their balance sheet as being their asset. In this situation, the public garage acts as the custodian of your car, while you retain ownership at all times.

With commercial banks the situation is entirely different. When you deposit currency coins or currency notes at your local bank, or when someone transfers digital money into your bank account; your deposit account will be reported as being a liability of the bank. This means that the bank owes you that money and that you are a

creditor to the bank. The bank is the legal owner of the money that you deposit with them. The only right that you have is a claim against the bank for the return of an equivalent sum of money.

With this in mind, let's look at the balance sheet of the Commonwealth Bank, where it clearly shows that client deposits as liabilities:

Liabilities		
Deposits and other public borrowings	17	543,231
Payables due to other financial institutions		36,416
Liabilities at fair value through Income Statement	18	8,493
Derivative liabilities	10	35,213

If you exercise your claim; the bank will meet your demand by giving you physical currency, or by transferring your deposit into a different account.

Regulations

The book Banking Regulation of UK and US Financial Markets by Dalvinder Singh (published 2007) provides elucidatory statements regarding the nature of deposits, and the legal position of depositors. On page 82 we find:

> The bank-customer relationship of **debtor and creditor** provides that a bank does not have a continuous obligation to account for its decisions as to how it uses depositors' money.

Page 83 informs us that depositors are unsecured creditors; implying that they are at the bottom of the totem pole during a period of liquidation:

> In general, **unsecured creditors, such as depositors of a bank**, will have very little redress to recover their debts if a company is put into liquidation.

Further on page 83, the author is explicit regarding the ownership of deposits:

> The money deposited in an account is no longer deemed as belonging to the principal **but rather to the bank**.

Devaynes vs Noble (1816)

The question of whether money deposited at a commercial bank belongs to the client or to the bank is not new. The issue has been tested in courts for over two centuries. In 1816 a judge in England stated the following in the case of Devaynes vs Noble:

 Money paid into a banker's becomes immediately a part of his general assets; and he is merely a debtor for the amount.

> Sir William Grant MR
> Court of Chancery
> 9 March 1816

In this case the judge is of the opinion that the bank is a debtor, and by implication that the client who deposited the money is a creditor.

Foley vs Hill (1848)

In 1848 the case of Edward Thomas Foley vs Thomas Hill reinforced the position that depositors are unsecured creditors, and that money deposited at a bank belongs to the bank. Lord Chancellor Cottenham said the following in his judgement:

> Money, when paid into a bank, ceases altogether to be the money of the principal; it is by then **the money of the banker**, who is bound to return an equivalent by paying a similar sum to that deposited with him when he is asked for it.

NB

The language is clear; if you deposit money at a bank – you no longer have a claim on the money, but only a claim against the bank for the return of an **equivalent sum**. The distinction that is being made is subtle, but it is very important.

Scammon vs Kimball (1875)

In October of 1875, Mr Justice Clifford (of the Circuit Court of the United States for the Northern District of Illinois) delivered his opinion in the case of Scammon vs Kimball, where he made direct reference to the earlier ruling of Devaynes vs Noble. Below is an extract from the court record:

> Authorities to the same effect are numerous and decisive; as, for example, it was expressly decided by the Master of the Rolls that **money paid to a banker becomes immediately a part of his general assets**, and he is merely a debtor for the amount. *Devaynes* v. *Noble*, 1 Meriv. 561.

The court record provides useful insight into the legal nature of money deposited at a bank, and clarifies the distinction between money held in custody (e.g. held in a safe deposit box) and money generally deposited (and recorded as a liability). In the context of the extract, a **bailee** is defined as a person to whom personal property is entrusted for a particular purpose:

> All deposits made with bankers, said Mr Justice Miller, may be divided into two classes: namely, those in which the bank becomes **bailee** of the depositor, the title to the thing deposited remaining with the latter; and that other kind of deposit of money, peculiar to banking business, in which **the depositor for his own convenience parts with the title of his money, and loans it to the banker**; and the latter, in consideration of the loan of the money and the right to use it for his own profit, agrees to refund the same amount, or any part thereof, on demand. *Marine Bank* v. *Fulton Bank*, 2 Wall. 256.

The extract is summarised as below:

- In the course of general banking – deposits are owned by the bank.
- Where the bank is a custodian – the deposit is owned by the client.

This situation is as relevant today as it was in 1875. The more things change, the more they stay the same (with apologies to Jean-Baptiste Alphonse Karr).

Reserve Bank of Australia

The Reserve Bank does not state explicitly that depositors are unsecured creditors. However, there are numerous documents published by the Reserve Bank that make this inference. For example, the December Quarterly Bulletin 2011 states the following on page 1:

> There are a number of reasons why authorities may seek to provide greater protection to **depositors than to other creditors** of banks.

The term "other creditors" clearly implies that depositors are creditors. On page 11 of the same document the following statement is found:

> This means that Australian depositors have a priority claim on the assets of a failed ADI (Authorised Deposit-taking Institution) ahead of **other unsecured creditors**.

Again, the term "other unsecured creditors" implies that depositors are unsecured creditors. From the extracts provided, it should be safe to conclude that depositors are unsecured creditors, and that deposits are owned by the bank.

No protection

The following extract is from the Reserve Bank web site:

> The Reserve Bank of Australia has responsibility for monetary policy and for overall financial system stability. The RBA has no obligation to protect the interests of bank depositors or other creditors of banks.

This extract states that the Reserve Bank has **no legal obligation to protect depositors** in Australia. This may shatter the generally held belief that somehow the Reserve Bank is a big brother looking after their monetary interest.

Chapter 16 :   The Central Bank

> The bank can create and destroy money. Bank credit is money. It's the money we do most of our business with, not with that currency we usually think of as currency.
>
> Mr Marriner Stoddard Eccles
> Former chairman of the Federal Reserve Board

The majority of the Australian public has a limited understanding of the role and function of the Reserve Bank of Australia. To them, the central bank is cloaked in reverence and articulates on matters supposedly beyond their comprehension. Hopefully this chapter will remedy that situation.

Legislation

The Reserve Bank was established by the Reserve Bank Act of 1959. Section 10(1) of the act states that the Reserve Bank Board has the power to set the policy of the Bank, while Section 10(2) states that such policy must be directed to the greatest advantage of the people of Australia:

> (2) It is the duty of the Reserve Bank Board, within the limits of its powers, to ensure that the monetary and banking policy of the Bank is directed to the greatest advantage of the people of Australia and that the powers of the Bank under this Act and any other Act, other than the *Payment Systems (Regulation) Act 1998,*

The section continues, and states that the policies of the Board must contribute to the attainment of three benchmarks. The Reserve Bank calls these three benchmarks the statutory objectives of the Board:

the *Payment Systems and Netting Act 1998* and Part 7.3 of the *Corporations Act 2001*, are exercised in such a manner as, in the opinion of the Reserve Bank Board, will best contribute to:

    (a) the <u>stability of the currency</u> of Australia;

    (b) the maintenance of <u>full employment</u> in Australia; and

    (c) the <u>economic prosperity and welfare</u> of the people of Australia.

The act does not state explicitly the issues that monetary policy should address. However, section 8 grants the Reserve Bank a list of powers to achieve its mandate. The most relevant are:

- To receive money on deposit.
- To lend money.
- To buy, sell, discount and re-discount bills of exchange, promissory notes and treasury bills.
- To buy and sell securities issued by the Commonwealth and other securities.
- To do anything incidental to any of its powers.

Setting interest rates

In Australia, reserve accounts are called Exchange Settlement accounts. People mistakenly believe that when central banks implement monetary policy they set a minimum amount of money to be held in such reserve accounts. The Bank of England articulates this misconception in their article Money Creation in the Modern Economy:

> This description of the relationship between monetary policy and money **differs from the description in many introductory textbooks**, where central banks determine the quantity of broad money via a "money multiplier" by actively varying the quantity of reserves.

The Bank of England points out on page 8 of their article that monetary policy is about setting interest rates:

> Central banks do not typically choose a quantity of reserves to bring about the desired short-term interest rate. Rather, **they focus on prices - setting interest rates**.

Peter Costello, the Treasurer of the Commonwealth of Australia from March 1996 to December 2007, is a bit more flamboyant in his description of what the Reserve Bank does:

> Now that both sides of politics have decided to crack down on the evil practice of price signalling, we may as well ask who does it and why. Some people may not be aware that the biggest price signaller is not the Commonwealth Bank or Westpac or any of the other "evil" commercial banks. **The biggest price signaller in the interest rate market is the Reserve Bank of Australia.**

> Peter Costello
> November 2010

Price inflation

The Reserve Bank provides an explanation of monetary policy on its web site:

> Monetary policy involves **setting the interest rate** on overnight loans in the money market (the cash rate). The cash rate influences other interest rates in the economy, affecting the behaviour of borrowers and lenders, economic activity and ultimately **the rate of inflation**.

The Reserve Bank also published the following diagram; which shows how a change in the cash rate (i.e. the rate on central bank money) permeates through the economy to have an effect on prices.

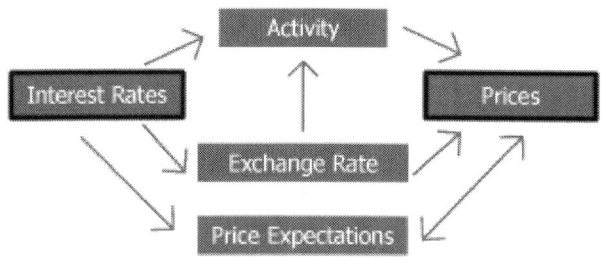

The Reserve Bank states that keeping price inflation within a narrow band achieves its statutory objectives (as listed above):

> To achieve these statutory objectives, the Bank has an inflation target and seeks to keep **consumer price inflation** in the economy to **2 to 3%** on average, over the medium term.

This is the ultimate objective of the Reserve Bank – control price inflation.

Transmission

The diagram above is generic, but can be of greater value if altered to display realistic links between interest rates and prices. To identify the links, we turn to the article Money Creation in the Modern Economy from the Bank of England.

The first link is between **interest rates** and **money creation** (on page four):

> The ultimate constraint on **money creation** is monetary policy. By influencing the level of **interest rates** in the economy, the Bank of England's monetary policy affects how much households and companies want to borrow ... Monetary policy acts as the ultimate limit on **money creation**.

The second link is between **money creation** and **prices** (on page one):

> The Bank of England aims to make sure the amount of **money creation** in the economy is consistent with low and stable **inflation**.

With the chain complete, we recast the transmission mechanism to better reflect the reality of our current monetary system.

Interest rates → Money creation → Prices

The detailed version of the transmission mechanism is below:

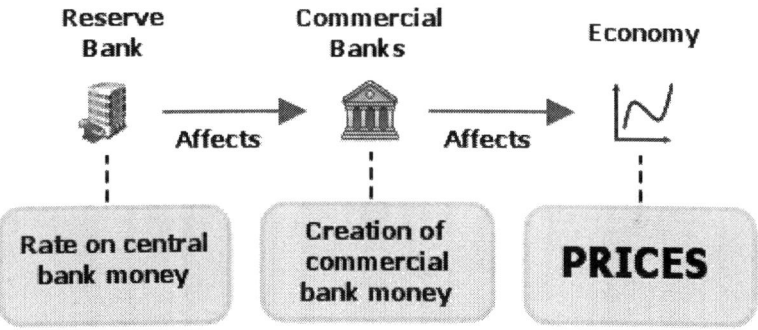

The transmission mechanism works as follows:

- The central bank lowers the rate on central bank money.
- Commercial banks lower the rate on commercial bank money.
- Cheaper money stimulates public borrowing.
- Additional money is created via debt monetisation.
- Monetary inflation increases price inflation.

Monetary policy

The cash rate on central bank money is set when the Reserve Bank Board meets (normally 11 times each year). After each meeting, a media release is issued which communicates their decision. One such release is provided below:

Statement by Philip Lowe, Governor: Monetary Policy Decision

Number   **2016-27**

Date   **1 November 2016**

At its meeting today, the Board decided to leave the cash rate unchanged at 1.50 per cent.

The cash rate in Australia has moved as follows:

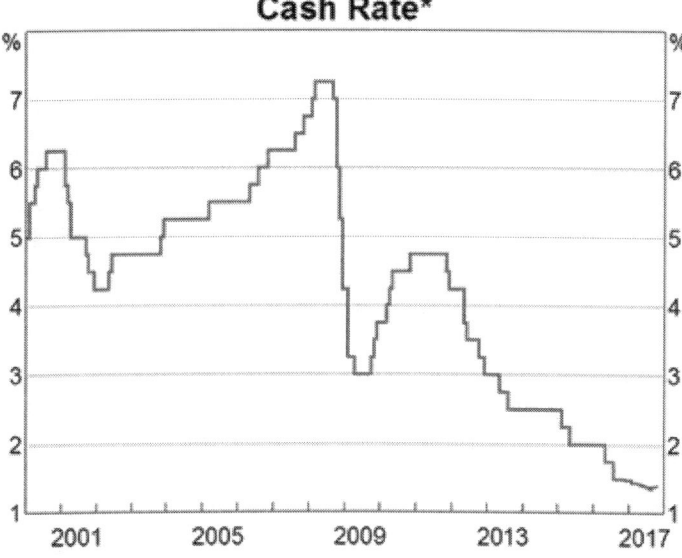

Cash Rate*

*   Data from December 2016 onwards are expectations derived from interbank cash rate futures

Sources: ASX; Bloomberg

Price inflation is a tax

The average Australian finds little wrong with price inflation in the 2 to 3% range. Many enterprises find price inflation to be a boon for their business, since a product bought today can be sold for more tomorrow. Yet, behind this veneer lies a cruel truth.

> Inflation is as violent as a mugger, as frightening as an armed robber and as deadly as a hit man.

> Ronald Reagan
> 40th President of the USA
> 1981 - 1989

The Reserve Bank was established in 1959. Below is a graph of the purchasing power of the Australian dollar since March 1960. The graph is based on the Consumer Price Index as obtained from the Australian Bureau of Statistics

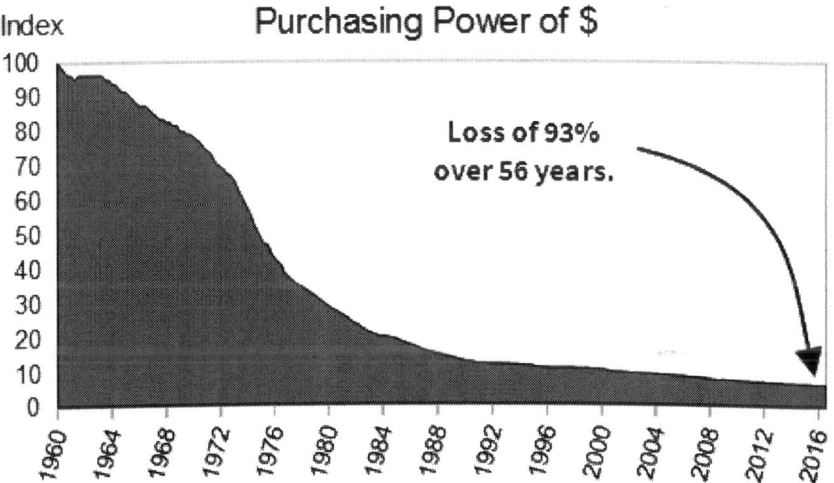

In March 1960 the index was at 100. In March 2016 the index was at 7. This is a 93% devaluation of the Australian dollar over 56 years. John Maynard Keynes (past director of the Bank of England) describes the effects of price inflation as follows:

> By a continuing process of **inflation**, governments can **confiscate**, secretly and unobserved, **an important part of the wealth of their citizens**. There is no subtler, no surer means of overturning the existing basis of society than to debauch the

currency. The process engages all the hidden forces of economic law on the side of destruction, and does it in a manner which not one man in a million is able to diagnose.

Confiscating a small portion of the wealth of the public each and every year, is no less distasteful than confiscating a large portion of their wealth in a single swoop. It is only the measure of pretence that differs.

Devaluation

When the price of a currency is quoted, it is done with reference to another currency. For example:

$$1.00 \text{ USD} = 0.899845 \text{ EUR}$$

US Dollar ↔ Euro

1 USD = 0.899845 EUR   1 EUR = 1.11130 USD

The impression is that one currency is stable while the other currency is rising or falling in value. The truth is that all currencies are falling in value due to the effects of monetary inflation and price inflation. The only difference between currencies is that some are losing their value faster than others.

Quoting currencies in this manner is akin to determining which ship is most seaworthy when all are taking on water. All currencies are fiat and heading in the same direction.

 Paper money eventually returns to its intrinsic value -- zero.

Voltaire
French writer, philosopher, playwright, and historian
1694 - 1778

Measure value

The proper way to measure a currency is against a basket of physical goods, or against a single asset such as gold. Such a comparison quickly highlights the fact that all currencies are on a downward trajectory. Below is a graph from Bullion Management Group Inc. that shows this concept rather well. The four currencies in the graphic are:

- US dollar
- Canadian dollar
- Euro
- UK pound

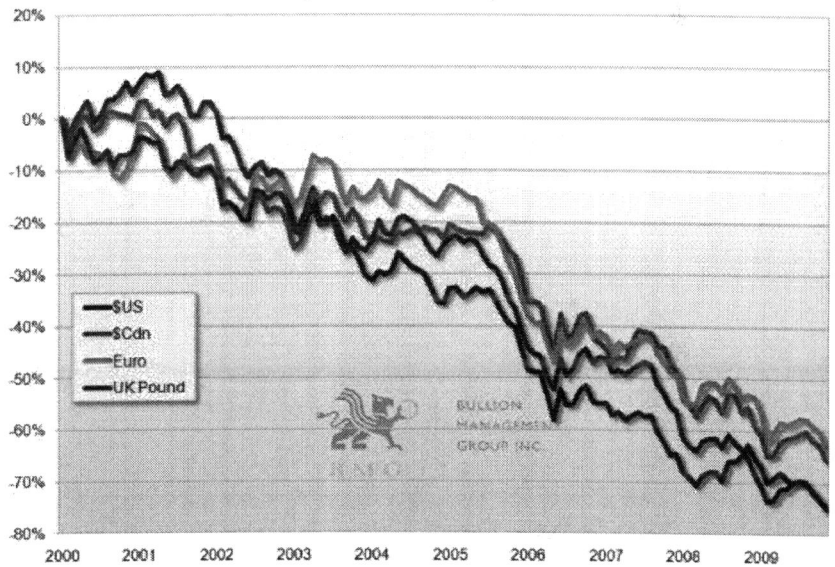

It matters little what the exchange rates between the currencies are; the long-term trend indicates that they are heading to their intrinsic value. Historically, the average life of a fiat currency is approximately 27 years. Within this context, it is safe to conclude that our debt-based monetary system is past its "use by date".

Preserve value

The Reserve Bank of Australia is legally bound to contribute to:

- The stability of the Australian currency.
- Full employment in Australia.
- The economic prosperity and welfare of Australians.

The Reserve Bank equates price inflation in the 2 to 3% range as meeting its statutory objectives. One of the objectives is to maintain the stability of the Australian currency. On their web site they state:

> **Controlling inflation preserves the value of money** and encourages strong and sustainable growth in the economy over the longer term.

With the knowledge that price inflation is a cruel and hidden tax, it is difficult to comprehend how the continual devaluation of a currency (which has already lost 93% of its value) contributes to the preservation of its value.

Chapter 17 : Exchange Settlement accounts

We are completely dependent on the commercial banks. Someone has to borrow every dollar we have in circulation, cash, or credit. If the banks create ample synthetic money, we are prosperous; if not, we starve.

Robert H. Hemphill
Credit Manager
Federal Reserve Bank of Atlanta Georgia

Money class

Two money classes are examined, namely central bank money and commercial bank money. The objective is to provide a simplified view of how Exchange Settlement accounts work.

Intra-bank payments

Intra-bank payments involve the transfer of funds between deposit accounts at the same bank. These transfers are made without involving Exchange Settlement accounts at the Reserve Bank.

For example, if Mr Green and Mrs Purple maintain deposit accounts at the same bank, and if Mr Green pays $100 to Mrs Purple; then the payment is processed as per the adjacent diagram. The $100 is transferred from one account to the other; without affecting the central bank.

| Mr Green | -$100 |
| Mrs Purple | +$100 |

Inter-bank payments

Inter-bank payments involve the transfer of funds between deposit accounts at different commercial banks. In this case the Exchange Settlement accounts of both banks are affected. For example, if Mr Green has an account at Bank A and pays $100 to Mrs Purple (who has an account at Bank B) then the payment is processed as follows:

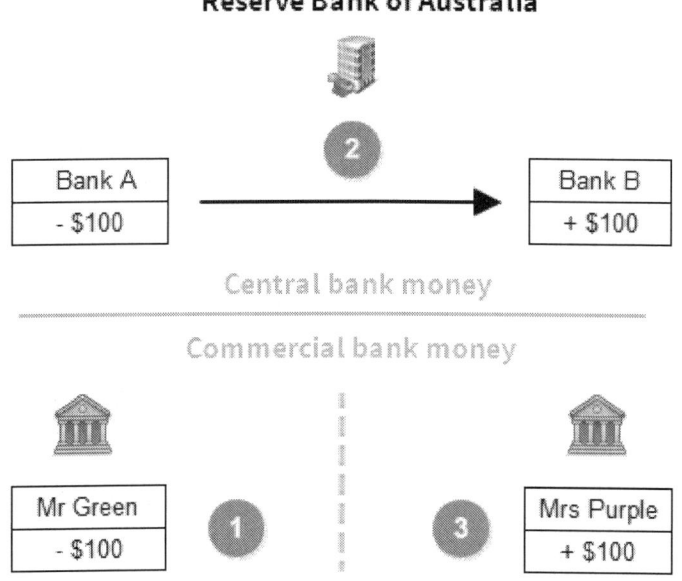

Inter-bank payments comprise three separate but related transactions; one at the payer bank, one at the central bank, and one at the receiving bank. The money used by the central bank is central bank money, while the money used by the commercial banks is commercial bank money. The three related transactions are:

1. Bank A deducts $100 from the account of Mr Green.
2. The central bank transfers $100 from Bank A to Bank B.
3. Bank B deposits $100 into the account of Mrs Purple.

Before continuing, we examine how Exchange Settlement accounts work.

How ES accounts work

There are two types of deposit accounts at the Reserve Bank of Australia, namely General Deposit accounts and Exchange Settlement accounts. In this chapter we only focus on Exchange Settlement accounts.

A Reserve Bank media release dated 1 March 1999 contains the following:

> Exchange Settlement accounts are the means by which providers of payments services **settle obligations** that have accrued in the clearing process.

The Reserve Bank published a document in March 1999 entitled The Role of Exchange Settlement Accounts, which points out that these accounts contain central bank money:

> The banks have merely used **central bank-issued money** to settle the obligations between themselves.

A logical question at this point is; how do commercial banks obtain central bank money?

Funding ES accounts

There is only one source for central bank money, and that is the Reserve Bank. Once a commercial bank has central bank money in an account, it can transfer the money to another commercial bank. In the Reserve Bank Annual Report 2014, we find the following:

> Authorised Deposit-taking Institutions [i.e. commercial banks] **fund these balances** using reverse repurchase agreements with the [central] Bank ...

Below is an example of how funding occurs. Assume a commercial bank owns a government bond valued at $1,000 and wants to convert it into central bank money. The initial balance sheet of the commercial bank looks as follows:

Commecial Bank A – Balance Sheet			
Assets		Liabilities	
Government bond	$1,000	Deposit – Mr Green	$1,000

The commercial bank sells the bond to the Reserve Bank for $1,000 of central bank money. The money is deposited into its Exchange Settlement account. The resulting balance sheet of the commercial bank is as follows:

Commecial Bank A – Balance Sheet			
Assets		Liabilities	
Cash at RBA	$1,000	Deposit – Mr Green	$1,000

The Reserve Bank monetises the bond, i.e. it records the bond as an asset and simultaneously creates $1,000 of central bank money. The new money is deposited into the Exchange Settlement account of the commercial bank. The balance sheet of the Reserve Bank looks as follows:

Reserve Bank of Australia – Balance Sheet			
Assets		Liabilities	
Government bond	$1,000	Deposit – Bank A	$1,000

Once the commercial bank has $1,000 of central bank money in its account, it is ready to make an inter-bank payment.

One: Payer bank

We return to our example where Mr Green pays $100 to Mrs Purple. The first transaction occurs at the payer bank. Bank A deducts $100 from the deposit account of Mr Green, and simultaneously records that its Exchange Settlement account (at the central bank) will be reduced by $100. The commercial bank balance sheet looks as follows:

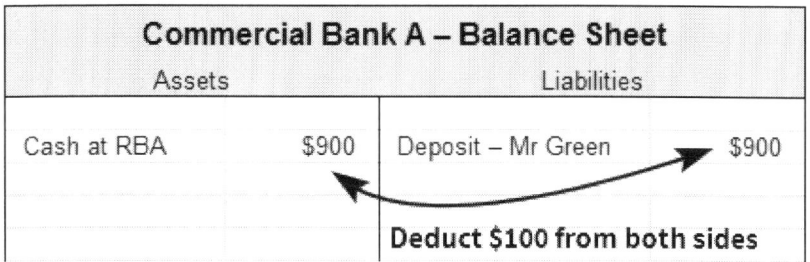

Commercial Bank A – Balance Sheet		
Assets		Liabilities
Cash at RBA	$900	Deposit – Mr Green $900
		Deduct $100 from both sides

Bank A sends a message to the Reserve Bank informing them of the payment.

Two: Central bank

The second transaction occurs at the central bank. The central bank transfers $100 (of central bank money) from the account of Bank A into the account of Bank B. The balance sheet of the Reserve Bank looks as follows:

Reserve Bank of Australia – Balance Sheet		
Assets		Liabilities
Government bond	$1,000	Deposit – Bank A $900
		Deposit – Bank B $100
		Transfer $100 of central bank money

The Reserve Bank sends a message to Bank B informing them that their Exchange Settlement account has been credited with $100 (of central bank money) and that they must credit the account of Mrs Purple with $100 (of commercial bank money).

Three: Receiving bank

The third transaction occurs at the receiving bank. Bank B records the deposit of $100 in their Exchange Settlement account, and simultaneously deposits $100 into the account of Mrs Purple. Their balance sheet looks as follows:

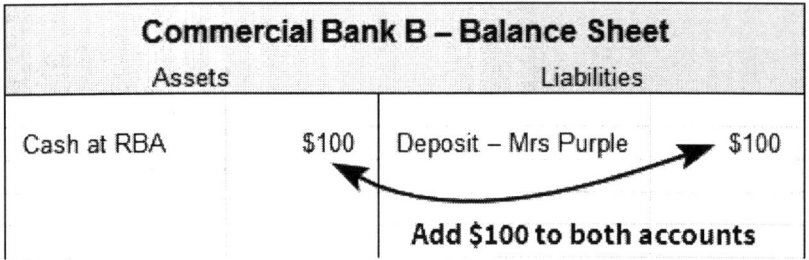

Commercial Bank B – Balance Sheet		
Assets		Liabilities
Cash at RBA	$100	Deposit – Mrs Purple $100
		Add $100 to both accounts

Once all three transactions are processed, the inter-bank payment is complete.

No overdrafts

From the Reserve Bank Annual Report 2014 we gather some additional information about the nature of Exchange Settlement accounts; such as the fact that they are not allowed to be overdrawn:

> ES account holders are **not permitted to overdraw their accounts**, although the Reserve Bank remains willing to advance funds overnight against eligible securities to account holders at an interest rate 25 basis points above the cash rate target. In general, this occurs only when banks have to meet unforeseen payments late in the day and are unable to source funds elsewhere.

Lending reserves

There is a common belief that commercial banks somehow lend the surplus deposits that they hold in their reserve accounts to the general public. This belief is false.

Below is a statement by Professor Scott Fullwiler (Associate Professor of Economics at Wartburg College) on the subject:

> Banks can't "do" anything with all the extra reserve balances. Loans create deposits - **reserve balances don't finance lending or add any "fuel" to the economy**. Banks don't lend reserve balances except in the federal funds market, and in that case the Fed always provides sufficient quantities to keep the federal funds rate at its ... interest rate target.

A number of important points are made in the statement. These are itemised below:

- Commercial banks monetise debts.
- Central bank money is only lent to commercial banks.
- Central bank money is not lent to the public.
- Reserves do not stimulate commercial bank lending.
- The central bank will lend as much money as needed to keep the rate on central bank money at the target level.

KEEP READING

Chapter 18 : Quantitative easing

QE is intended to boost the amount of money in the economy directly by purchasing assets, mainly from non-bank financial companies.

Bank of England
Money creation in the modern economy
2014

Terminology

Quantitative easing is the most convoluted phrase ever designed to confuse and mislead the public. Since quantitative easing has yet to reach the shores of Australia, neutral terminology will be employed.

Money classes

There are two money classes involved in QE transactions, namely central bank money and commercial bank money. To date we have observed how:

- Commercial bank money is increased when a commercial bank monetises a debt.
- Central bank money is increased when a central bank monetises a financial security.

QE is an odd combination of both transactions. When a central bank executes a QE transaction, it increases the quantity of both central bank money and commercial bank money. The counterparty to the central bank is not a commercial bank, but rather a **non-bank** entity, i.e. an entity that does not maintain a reserve account at the central bank.

Objective

The Bank of England sets out the objective of QE in their article Quantitative Easing from their Second Quarterly Bulletin 2009:

> The aim of quantitative easing is to **inject money into the economy** in order to revive nominal spending.

The Bank points out that an increase in commercial bank money eventually leads to price inflation:

> Increases in money should eventually lead to a **rise in prices**.

In their article Money Creation in the Modern Economy, they combine these two ideas as follows:

> QE initially **increases the amount of bank deposits** those [non-bank] companies hold (in place of the assets they sell). Those [non-bank] companies will then wish to rebalance their portfolios of assets by buying higher-yielding assets, **raising the price of those assets** and **stimulating spending** in the economy.

We can conclude that the objective of quantitative easing is to:

- Increase prices (i.e. price inflation).
- Increase public spending (i.e. increase GDP).

Mechanism

The article Quantitative Easing provides the following information:

> This means that while asset purchases from banks increase the monetary base (or "narrow money"), purchases from non-banks **increase the monetary base and broad money at the same time**.

It is clear that when a central bank monetises a financial security tendered by a non-bank entity, that the quantity of both central bank money and commercial bank is increased. The idea is repeated further in the article:

[Commercial] banks gain both **new reserves** and a corresponding **new customer deposit** when assets are purchased [by the central bank] from non-banks.

Diagrammatically this is presented as follows:

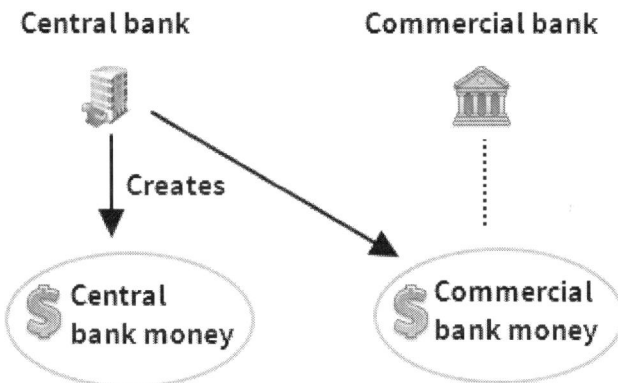

To explain how QE works, an example is provided. Assume a non-bank entity called Hedge Fund owns a government bond valued at $1,000. The entity does not have a reserve account, but it does have a deposit account at a commercial bank, namely ABC Bank. The QE program involves three parties.

One: The central bank

The central bank initiates the transaction when it buys the bond from the Hedge Fund. The central bank monetises the bond; i.e. it records the bond as an asset and simultaneously creates new central bank money. Since the Hedge Fund does not have a reserve account, the central bank deposits the $1,000 into the account of ABC Bank. The result is below:

Central Bank – Balance Sheet			
Assets		Liabilities	
Government bond	$1,000	Deposit – ABC Bank	$1,000

The central bank informs ABC Bank that its reserve account is credited with $1,000 of central bank money, and that it should credit the deposit account of the Hedge Fund with $1,000.

Two: The commercial bank

The commercial bank credits the deposit account of the Hedge Fund with $1,000 of commercial bank money and simultaneously records the increase of its cash account at the central bank. The balance sheet of ABC Bank looks as follows:

ABC Bank – Balance Sheet			
Assets		Liabilities	
Cash at Central Bank	$1,000	Deposit – Hedge Fund	$1,000

Three: The non-bank entity

Prior to the transaction, the Hedge Fund owned a government bond. Its balance sheet looked as follows:

Hedge Fund – Balance Sheet			
Assets		Liabilities	
Government bond	$1,000	Some liabilities	$1,000

Following the sale of the bond to the central bank, the Hedge Fund has $1,000 in its deposit account.

Hedge Fund – Balance Sheet			
Assets		Liabilities	
Cash at ABC Bank	$1,000	Some liabilities	$1,000

The Hedge Fund can now purchase other assets with the $1,000. The statement by the Bank of England is worth repeating:

> Those [non-bank] companies will then wish to rebalance their portfolios of assets by buying higher-yielding assets, **raising the price of those assets** and **stimulating spending** in the economy.

Double new money

Quantitative easing is implemented in three steps and results in an increase of both central bank money and commercial bank money. The three steps are:

- Central bank buys asset from non-bank entity.
- Central bank creates new money.
- Commercial bank creates new money
  (under instruction from the central bank).

The diagram below provides a simplified view of a quantitative easing transaction.

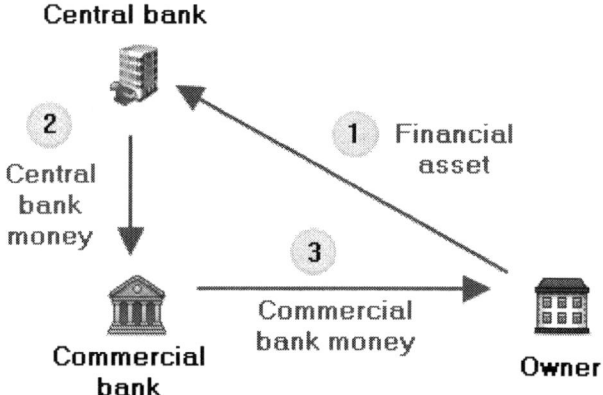

The amount of money created via QE programs in the USA is staggering. The Federal Reserve reports that it has created approximately $2.8 trillion of new central bank money (and simultaneously $2.8 trillion of new commercial bank money).

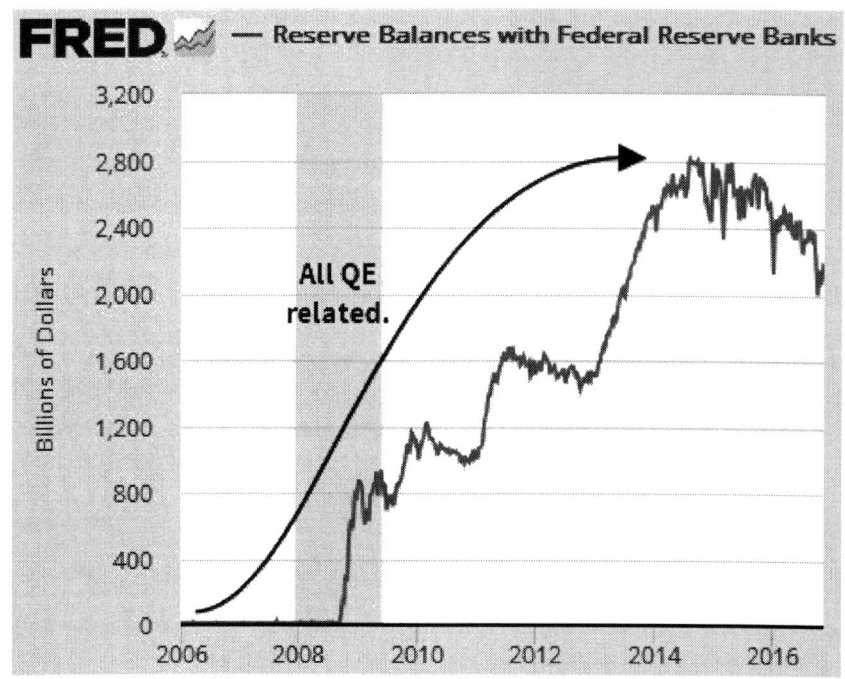

Easy interest

The central bank receives interest from the issuer of the financial asset. The commercial bank receives interest from the central bank due to its deposit account at the central bank. The depositor receives interest from the commercial bank due on its deposit account at the commercial bank. In a nutshell, interest payments move between the parties as follows:

1. The bond issuer pays interest to the central bank.
2. The central bank pays interest to the commercial bank.
3. The commercial bank pays interest to the depositor.

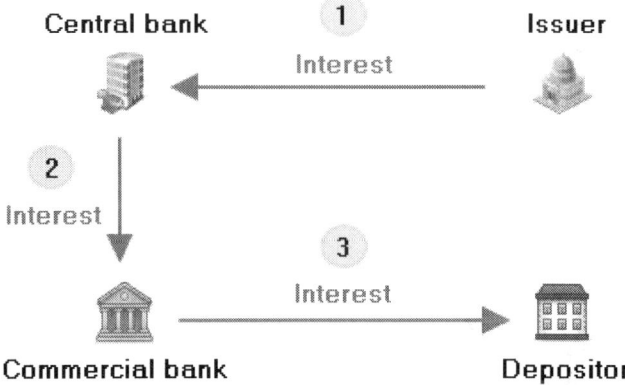

Interest paid to each subsequent party is obviously less than what is received.

Comparison

In our example, the central bank monetised a financial asset that was owned by a non-bank entity. The end result is an increase of $1,000 in central bank money and an increase of $1,000 in commercial bank money.

Below is a table that provides a comparative view of normal central bank lending versus quantitative easing. To date quantitative easing has been implemented by the Federal Reserve, the Bank of England, the European Central Bank and the Bank of Japan.

	Normal lending	Quantitative easing
Central Bank monetises a	financial security	financial security
tendered by a	commercial bank	non-bank entity
which has	a reserve account.	no reserve account.
The term is	short (days).	long (outright).
This increases	central bank money.	central bank money & commercial bank money.
Monetary inflation	-	Higher
Price inflation	-	Higher
GDP	-	Higher

Summary

Monetary policy allows central banks to set interest rates on central bank money. This affects money creation at the commercial bank level, which in turn affects prices. The objective of central banks is to keep price inflation in a defined range (e.g. 2 to 3%).

Quantitative easing provides an additional lever to central banks with which to meet their objective. It gives them the ability to directly alter the quantity of commercial bank money in the economy. By controlling the quantity of money, central banks hope to not only affect prices, and also gross domestic product.

Chapter 19 : Banks buy currency

Banks do not create money for the public good. They are businesses owned by private shareholders. Their purpose is to make a profit.

John Rogers
Local Money: What Difference Does It Make?

Money classes

There are two money classes involved when commercial banks buy notes from the central bank. They are central bank money and currency notes - which are printed and issued by the Reserve Bank of Australia.

Central bank money

The Reserve Bank points out on its web site that when commercial banks buy currency notes, they pay with central bank money:

> When Authorised Deposit-taking Institutions **purchase banknotes from the Reserve Bank, settlement is in Exchange Settlement funds.**

Commercial banks can only obtain central bank money when they sell financial securities to the Reserve Bank (as part of a repurchase agreement). All repurchase agreements have an interest component. This means that there is a cost attached to commercial banks purchasing currency notes.

Commercial bank

By way of example; assume that a commercial bank has the following balance sheet, and that it needs to purchase $1,000 of currency notes:

Commercial Bank – Balance Sheet			
Assets		Liabilities	
Government bond	$1,000	Some liabilities	$1,000

To buy currency notes the commercial bank needs central bank money. It obtains the money by selling the bond to the Reserve Bank for $1,000. After the sale, the commercial bank balance sheet looks as follows:

Commercial Bank – Balance Sheet			
Assets		Liabilities	
Cash at RBA	$1,000	Some liabilities	$1,000

The commercial bank now buys the currency notes and pays with central bank money. After the purchase, the commercial bank balance sheet looks as follows:

Commercial Bank – Balance Sheet			
Assets		Liabilities	
Currency notes	$1,000	Some liabilities	$1,000

The commercial bank can now place these notes into their automatic teller machines.

Central bank

The Reserve Bank monetises the government bond, i.e. it records the bond as an asset and simultaneously creates money that it deposits into the account of the commercial bank.

Reserve Bank of Australia – Balance Sheet			
Assets		Liabilities	
Government bond	$1,000	Deposit – Comm bank	$1,000

The Reserve Bank will print the currency notes, and then sell the notes to the commercial bank for $1,000. Following the sale, the balance sheet of the Reserve Bank looks as follows:

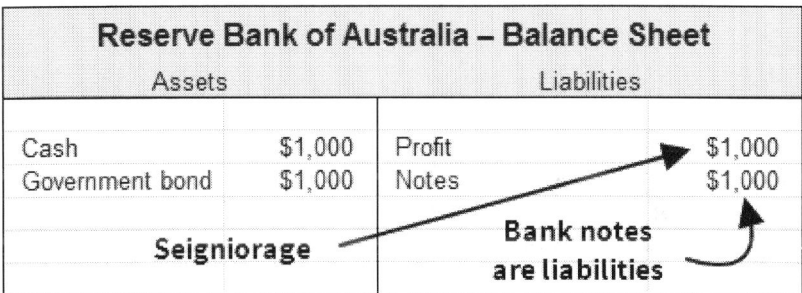

Reserve Bank of Australia – Balance Sheet			
Assets		Liabilities	
Cash	$1,000	Profit	$1,000
Government bond	$1,000	Notes	$1,000

Seigniorage

Bank notes are liabilities

In the Reserve Bank of Australia Annual Report for 2015, we see that it had $65.48 billion of Australian notes (i.e. currency notes) on issue:

Liabilities		
Deposits	1(b), 9	60,486
Distribution payable to the Commonwealth	1(g), 3	2,501
Australian notes on issue	1(b), 15	65,481
Other liabilities	10	4,576
Total Liabilities		133,044

Cost of notes

Commercial banks do not pay interest to members of the public on their holdings of currency notes. However, the Reserve Bank does pay interest to the commercial banks on their holdings of currency notes. Below is an extract from the Reserve Bank of Australia Annual Report 2015, which shows that commercial banks received 2.1% interest on their holdings of bank notes.

Interest expense		
Exchange Settlement balances	506	2.3
Deposits from governments	655	2.4
Deposits from overseas institutions	13	1.1
Banknote holdings of banks	63	2.1
Foreign repurchase agreements	(2)	(0.1)

The report also shows that the Reserve Bank received 2% interest on the repurchase agreements with commercial banks.

	Interest	Average annual interest rate
	$M	%
Interest revenue		
Foreign investments	148	0.3
Australian dollar investments	2,006	2.7
Overnight settlements	7	2.1
Cash collateral provided	3	2.3
Gold loans	—	0.3
Loans, advances and other	1	2.0

Eliminate cash

The call to eliminate cash (i.e. notes and coins) is growing louder. An article in The Telegraph dated 13 May 2015 suggests that cash should be made illegal to end boom and bust business cycles.

The Telegraph

Home Video News World Sport Finance Comment Culture Travel Life Women Fa

Companies Comment Personal Finance ISAs Economy Markets Property Enterprise

ISAs Investing | Pensions Savings | Interest Rates | Funds Mortgages | Credit Cards | Expat

HOME » FINANCE » PERSONAL FINANCE » COMMENT

How to end boom and bust: make cash illegal

Comment: Forcing everyone to spend only by electronic means from an account held at a government-run bank would give the authorities far better tools to deal with recessions and economic booms, writes Jim Leaviss

Two reasons are advanced, namely that it would ease the administrative and financial burden on banks, and that it would stimulate the economy.

> Officially, the aim is to ease "administrative and financial burdens", such as the cost of hiring a security service to send cash to the bank, and is part of a programme of reforms aimed at boosting growth – there is evidence that high cash usage in an economy acts as a drag.

While this argument has some merit, the article then veers into an Orwellian world where the government will **encourage** individuals on how to spend their money:

> And once all money exists only in bank accounts – monitored, or even directly controlled by the government – the authorities will be able to encourage us to spend more when the economy slows, or spend less when it is overheating

From this extract alone, it seems that the objective of eliminating cash is for government to control all privately held money.

Australia

In December 2016 the Australian government joined the chorus by calling for the elimination of the $100 note.

economy ▶ australian economy

Government floats $100 note removal

The reasons advanced are more considered, and are reproduced below:

- Reducing crime.
- Increasing tax revenue.
- Reducing welfare fraud.

Regardless of the noble sentiment, it is unlikely that eliminating a specific bank note will reform criminals, reduce crime and increase tax compliance. Perhaps addressing the source of crime is more logical.

Global

Globally, the war on cash is progressing as follows:

- USA: Policymakers are pushing to abolish $50 and $100 notes.
- Venezuela: The government has banned 100 bolivar note.
- Norway: DNB Bank proposed a ban on cash in 2016.
- Sweden: Banks have started removing ATMs from rural areas.
- France: Considering banning cash for transaction over €1,000.
- Europe: The ECB has stopped producing €500 notes.
- Greece: Citizens must declare all cash over €15,000 in safes.
- South Korea: Aims to eliminate paper money by 2020.
- Singapore: Eliminated the $10,000 in 2014.
- India: Demonetised the 500 and 1,000 rupee note.

Negative rates

On 10 February 2016, Zerohedge published an article entitled "Something very disturbing spotted in a Morgan Stanley presentation". The following extract sets out a more realistic objective for eliminating cash.

> We [the commercial banks] should move quickly to a cashless economy so that we can introduce negative interest rates well below 1%.

The term **negative interest rate** only applies to deposit balances at commercial banks, and not to the rate that commercial banks charge when they advance loans. This means that if a client borrows money from a bank, they will pay interest on the loan (as they normally do). If they deposit that money into an account, they will end up paying interest (via a negative interest rate) instead of receiving interest.

In other words – commercial banks intend to earn interest twice on the same amount of money; once when it is lent and again when it is deposited.

Bank runs

There is another reason why commercial banks want to eliminate cash. While currency notes are in use, depositors can theoretically demand that all of the money in their deposit accounts be paid out in the form of currency notes.

As at September 2016, there was approximately $1.83 trillion in deposit accounts in Australia. If depositors start withdrawing their money in the form of currency notes, commercial banks will be thrown into turmoil as they scramble to acquire central bank money (by entering into repurchase agreements with the central bank) in order to purchase currency notes.

Additionally, the financial securities (e.g. government bonds) that they need for their repurchase transactions will become scarce very quickly, sending their prices soaring. The end result is commercial banks being unable to secure sufficient central bank money. This is the definition of the banking industry being **illiquid**.

Bail-ins

The objective of eliminating cash is to leave the public with only a single money class at its disposal, namely commercial bank money.

Eliminating cash may reduce the probability of bank runs, but it does mean that depositors will have their monetary wealth trapped within the banking system. If a bank shows any sign of collapse; all a depositor can do is transfer their money to another bank. With the inter-connected nature of our banking system, it is unlikely that a single bank failure will leave others unscathed.

Once cash is eliminated, depositors will be reluctant participants in bank bail-ins. Simple mathematics dictates that bails-ins will occur in the future.

Chapter 20 : Cash and deposits

Neither paper currency nor deposits have value as commodities. Intrinsically, a dollar bill is just a piece of paper. Deposits are merely book entries.

Modern Money Mechanics
Federal Reserve of Chicago
1975

Money classes

In this chapter we examine how commercial banks report on their use of:

- Currency coins.
- Currency notes.
- Commercial bank money.
- Central bank money.

Balance sheet

Below is a simplified view of a commercial bank balance sheet, which is referenced throughout this chapter.

Commercial Bank – Balance Sheet					
Assets			Liabilities		
Notes	1	$1,000	Deposits	5	$4,000
Coins	2	$1,000			
Cash at banks	3	$1,000			
Cash at RBA	4	$1,000			

Notes and coins

Items #1 and #2 refer to currency notes and currency coins respectively. These two money classes are assets, and often reported as being **Cash**. Below is an extract from the ANZ Annual Report 2015.

Assets
Cash
Settlement balances owed to ANZ
Collateral paid
Trading securities

The entry for Cash is itemised below, with coins and notes at the top of the list.

10: Cash

Coins, notes and cash at bank
Money at call, bills receivable and remittances in transit
Securities purchased under agreements to resell in less than three months
Balances with Central Banks

Total cash

Cash at banks

Item #3 refers to digital money that the bank owns (and which was created via debt monetisation). Recall that digital money created by a commercial bank is called "commercial bank money" and digital money created by a central bank is called "central bank money".

Commercial banks record all client deposits as a liability. This means that the bank has a legal obligation to the owner of the deposit account. If a commercial bank owns digital money; it cannot deposit that money into a deposit account at one of its own branches. To do so means that it would have a legal obligation to itself – which is a legal nonsense. The only way a bank can deposit digital money that it owns is to deposit such money into a **deposit account at a different bank**.

In diagrammatic form this can be seen as below:

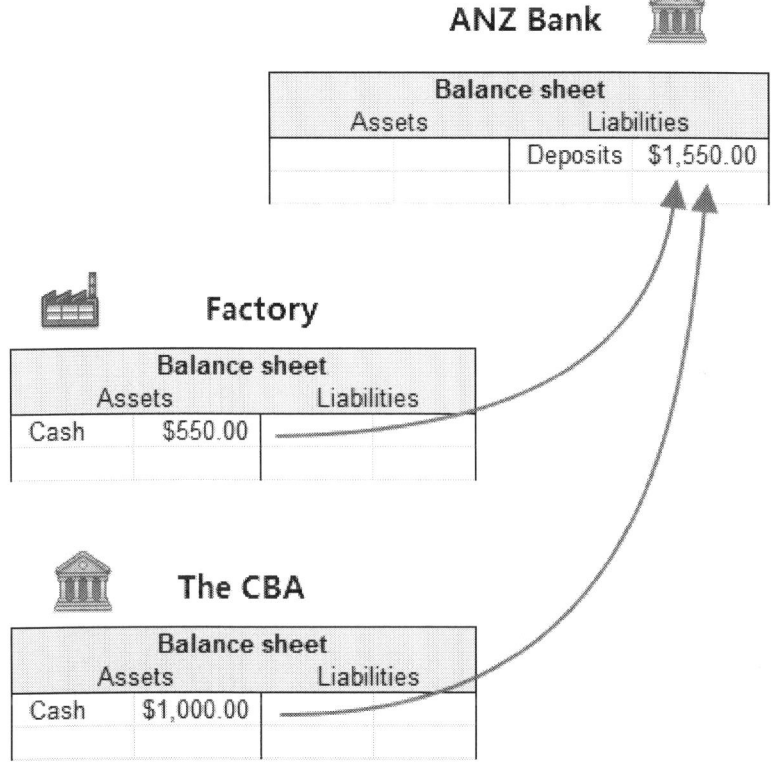

Actual example

The annual report of The Commonwealth Bank for 2015 shows an entry for cash and liquid assets.

	Note	2015 $M
Assets		
Cash and liquid assets	7	33,116
Receivables due from other financial institutions	8	11,540

This entry is itemised in note #7 of their annual report as below.

Note 7 Cash and Liquid Assets

	2015
	$M
Notes, coins and cash at banks	15,683
Money at short call	3,478
Securities purchased under agreements to resell	13,846
Bills received and remittances in transit	109
Total cash and liquid assets	33,116

The first entry includes **cash at banks**, with a healthy balance of $15.68 billion. This figure is close to their annual net interest income of $15.7 billion.

Deposits

Item #5 is commercial bank money and is recorded as a liability. In the annual report of the ANZ Bank for 2015 we find the following:

Liabilities
Settlement balances owed by ANZ
Collateral received
Deposits and other borrowings
Derivative financial instruments

Deposits from banks

The highlighted entry is itemised in note #16 of their annual report. Of particular interest is **Deposits from banks** (as shown below). This entry records the digital money that other banks have deposited into accounts maintained at the ANZ Bank.

16: Deposits and Other Borrowings

Certificates of deposit
Term Deposits
On demand and short term deposits
Deposits not bearing interest
Deposits from banks
Commercial Paper
Securities sold under repurchase agreements
Borrowing corporations[1]

Referring back to the diagram (two pages prior), the ANZ Bank would report the following:

- Deposits $1,550 (Factory and The CBA).
- Deposits from banks $1,000 (The CBA).

Central bank money

Item #4 is a record of the money that banks hold at the central bank, i.e. at the Reserve Bank of Australia. Unfortunately, commercial banks seldom provide a single figure of this cash balance. It is most likely that this cash balance is included in the figure of **Cash at banks**.

Since banks are constantly lending and borrowing central bank money between themselves, they do provide a snapshot of their obligations. In The CBA Annual Report 2015 we see that they are owed $11.5 billion and simultaneously owe $36.4 billion to other financial institutions.

Assets		
Cash and liquid assets	7	33,116
Receivables due from other financial institutions	8	11,540
Assets at fair value through Income Statement:	9	
Liabilities		
Deposits and other public borrowings	17	543,231
Payables due to other financial institutions		36,416

Terminology

When examining the annual report of commercial banks, it is useful to keep in mind the meaning of the following terms:

Notes & coins: This is physical currency notes and currency coins. They are recorded as assets.

Cash at banks: This is digital money that has been deposited at other commercial banks or at the central bank. Cash is recorded as an asset.

Deposits: This is commercial bank money, which is digital and which has been created via debt monetisation. Deposits are used in the economy to pay for goods and services. Deposits are recorded as liabilities.

Chapter 21 : Commercial bank profits

The real story is the commercial banks generating money and making profit for themselves by creating debt.

Professor Steve Keen
University of Western Sydney
Interviewed by Chris Martenson on 8 June 2012

Approach

The statement above by Professor Steve Keen encapsulates the process by which commercial banks generate profit. As documented in prior chapters; commercial banks monetise debt and then charge clients interest on the debt outstanding.

This chapter provides a generic explanation of how commercial banks charge interest (it being their principal source of revenue) and how payments are processed when clients settle the interest charge. Different commercial banks may have slightly different approaches, but the principle that is elucidated is the same.

Interest income

The Commonwealth Bank Annual Report for 2015 shows that the bulk of their revenue is interest income. Their net interest income of $15.7 billion is 76% of their total net operating income.

Income Statements

For the year ended 30 June 2015

	Note	2015 $M
Interest income	2	34,100
Interest expense	2	(18,305)
Net interest income		15,795
Other banking income		4,856
Net banking operating income		20,651

Cash

When a commercial bank charges interest on a loan, the bank records the revenue as **interest income**. When the client makes a payment to settle the interest charge, the bank records the receipt as **cash**. Cash is always reported as an asset (as shown below):

	Note	2015 $M
Assets		
Cash and liquid assets	7	33,116
Receivables due from other financial institutions	8	11,540
Assets at fair value through Income Statement	9	

Property loans

On 15 April 2015 the Australian Broadcasting Corporation published an article entitled "Australian banks' mortgage concentration worries analysts" where they state:

> Banks have 60% of their loan portfolios in housing.

The same article quotes a bank analyst as saying:

> … as far as I can work out the return on equity could be anywhere between 40 to 70%.

The numbers imply that the business of lending money to people to buy property is highly profitable. Some interesting numbers emerge when modelling a bank loan of $100,000 with monthly repayments over 20 years. At 7.95% the total amount of interest that the bank receives is equal to the value of the loan. Below are the first few rows of the spread sheet.

	Loan	Interest 7.95%	Loan & Interest	Repayment
1	$100,000	$663	$100,663	$833
2	$99,829	$661	$100,491	$833
3	$99,657	$660	$100,317	$833
4	$99,484	$659	$100,143	$833
5	$99,310	$658	$99,968	$833

The last few rows are given below. As shown, the sum of all interest payments equal $100,000. This means that the borrower pays double the listed price of the property.

236	$4,085	$27	$4,112	$833
237	$3,279	$22	$3,301	$833
238	$2,467	$16	$2,484	$833
239	$1,650	$11	$1,661	$833
240	$828	$5	$833	$833
	TOTAL	$100,000		$200,000

The rate of 7.95% is not exorbitant by any means. If the rate was higher or the loan was for 30 years; the bank would earn even more interest on the loan. A graph of mortgage rates in Australia is provided below:

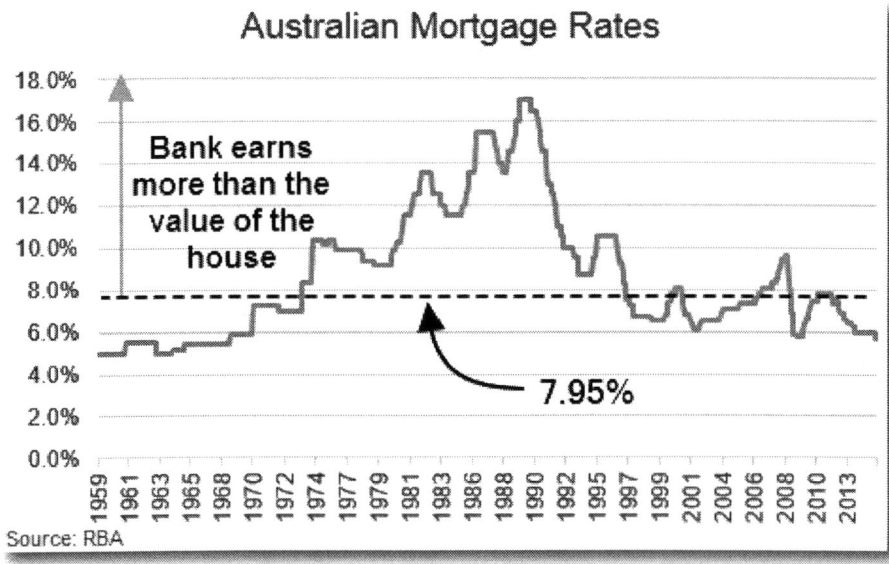

Australian Mortgage Rates

Source: RBA

Advance the loan

When a commercial bank lends money, it posts a journal entry to record a new loan (an asset) and the new deposit (a liability). This transaction does not affect the cash balance of the bank, and neither does it affect the deposit account of any other client.

By way of example; assume a commercial bank starts with $5,000 of equity and it lends $100,000 to Mr Green. The journal entry to record the loan is below:

Commercial Bank – Journal			
	Account	Debits	Credits
Dr	Loan – Mr Green	$100,000	
Cr	Deposit - Mr Green		$100,000

Once the entry is posted, the bank balance sheet looks as follows:

Commercial Bank – Balance Sheet			
Assets		Liabilities	
Government bond	$5,000	Equity	$5,000
Loan – Mr Green	$100,000	Deposit – Mr Green	$100,000
New loan		New deposit	

Charge interest

The commercial bank charges Mr Green interest of $5,000. The journal entry to record the interest is below. This entry is no different to what non-banking entities use when charging a debtor with interest.

Commercial Bank – Journal			
	Account	Debits	Credits
Dr	Loan – Mr Green	$5,000	
Cr	Interest income		$5,000

The result is an increase in the loan by $5,000 and an increase in interest income by $5,000. The interest income is displayed in the Income Statement and then flows into the Balance Sheet. Once the transaction is complete, the balance sheet looks as follows:

Commercial Bank – Balance Sheet		
Assets		Liabilities
Government bond	$5,000	Equity	$5,000
		Interest income	$5,000
Loan – Mr Green	$105,000	Deposit – Mr Green	$100,000
Interest charged but not yet paid		**Income on loan**	

Pay interest

In our example, Mr Green decides to pay the interest with some of the money in his deposit account. At this point we encounter a problem, since the bank cannot move $5,000 from the client deposit account into its own cash account in one step.

The reason for this is simple; the deposit account is a liability (it appears on the right hand side of the balance sheet), while the bank cash account is an asset (it appears on the left hand side of the balance sheet).

The problem is presented in a diagram below:

Commercial Bank – Balance Sheet

Assets		Liabilities	
Government bond	$5,000	Equity	$5,000
Cash at banks	-	Interest income	$5,000
Loan – Mr Green	$105,000	Deposit – Mr Green	$100,000

Cannot move $5,000.

Accounts are on different sides of balance sheet.

Recall that commercial banks maintain deposit accounts at other banks. The reason for this arrangement will now become clear.

Account at another bank

The solution for the bank is to move the $5,000 from the liability side of its balance sheet to the asset side in three steps – by utilising its deposit account at another bank. The three steps are:

1. Withdraw funds from deposit account.
2. Make inter-bank payment.
3. Record deposit at another bank.

What is described below may vary from bank to bank depending on their accounting practice. However, the general concept remains the same. What commercial banks do is transfer money from client deposit accounts (a liability) to their own deposit account held at another bank (also a liability) using the inter-bank payment mechanism.

One: Withdraw funds

The first step is for the commercial bank to withdraw $5,000 from the deposit account of Mr Green (as per his instruction), and to place it in a suspense account. The suspense account is merely a temporary account used to facilitate the payment. The result is shown below:

Commercial Bank – Balance Sheet			
Assets		Liabilities	
Government bond	$5,000	Equity	$5,000
Cash at banks	-	Interest income	$5,000
Loan – Mr Green	$105,000	Deposit – Mr Green	$95,000
		Suspense account	$5,000

Two: Inter-bank payment

The second step is for the commercial bank to make an inter-bank payment to another bank where it maintains its own deposit account. For the purpose of this example, assume that the commercial bank has a deposit account at a bank called the Other Bank.

To make inter-bank payments, commercial banks need central bank money. The commercial bank obtains central bank money by selling its government bond to the Reserve Bank of Australia under a repurchase agreement. Once done, the commercial bank balance sheet looks as follows:

Commercial Bank – Balance Sheet			
Assets		Liabilities	
Government bond	-	Equity	$5,000
Cash at RBA	$5,000	Interest income	$5,000
Loan – Mr Green	$105,000	Deposit – Mr Green	$95,000
		Suspense account	$5,000

As discussed in a prior chapter; inter-bank payments involve three separate but related transactions. The commercial bank initiates the payment by deducting $5,000 from its cash account at the Reserve Bank, and also deducting $5,000 from the suspense account.

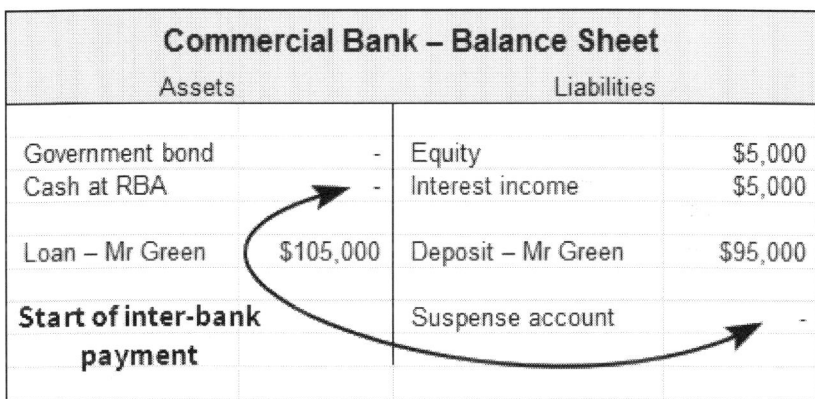

Commercial Bank – Balance Sheet			
Assets		Liabilities	
Government bond	-	Equity	$5,000
Cash at RBA	-	Interest income	$5,000
Loan – Mr Green	$105,000	Deposit – Mr Green	$95,000
Start of inter-bank payment		Suspense account	-

The remaining two transactions of the inter-bank payment are:

- The central bank transfers $5,000 from the commercial bank to the Other Bank.
- The Other Bank credits the deposit account of the commercial bank.

The last transaction of the inter-bank payment results in the balance sheet of the Other Bank looking as follows:

Other Bank – Balance Sheet		
Assets	**Liabilities**	
Cash at RBA $5,000	Deposit – Comm Bank	$5,000
Deposit account of commercial bank at "other bank"		

Three: Record deposit

Once the inter-bank payment is complete, the commercial bank records the movement of the deposit and the reduction of the loan in the journal entry below:

Commercial Bank – Journal			
	Account	Debits	Credits
Dr	Cash at banks	$5,000	
Cr	Loan – Mr Green		$5,000

The commercial bank balance sheet reflects the deposit of $5,000 in its own account, along with a $5,000 reduction in the loan.

Commercial Bank – Balance Sheet			
Assets		**Liabilities**	
Cash at banks $5,000		Equity	$5,000
Interest paid		Interest income	$5,000
Loan – Mr Green	$100,000	Deposit – Mr Green	$95,000

Total deposits

In our example, the total amount of commercial bank money remains at $100,000. What occurred is that $5,000 of commercial bank money has been moved to another bank, namely the Other Bank. The total amount of commercial bank money is split over two banks, namely:

- $95,000 at the commercial bank.
- $5,000 at the Other Bank.

Suspense account

Commercial banks may process these transactions differently. Some may even call their suspense account by a different name, such as **shadow cash** account or **daily cash movement** account. Regardless of name, the account is particularly useful when used to aggregate multiple client payments into a single inter-bank payment.

Before

It is instructive to examine the balance sheet of the commercial bank prior to the interest charge, and once again after the interest is paid. The before balance sheet looks as follows:

Commercial Bank – Balance Sheet			
Assets		Liabilities	
Government bond	$5,000	Equity	$5,000
Cash at banks	-	Interest income	-
Loan – Mr Green	$100,000	Deposit – Mr Green	$100,000

After

The after balance sheet looks as follows:

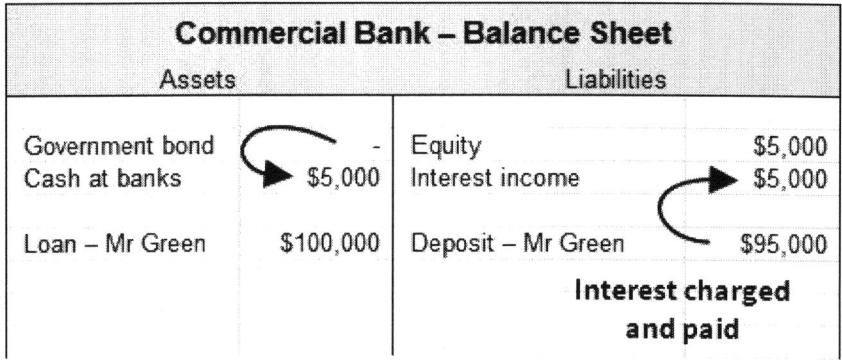

Commercial Bank – Balance Sheet		
Assets	**Liabilities**	
Government bond	-	Equity	$5,000
Cash at banks	$5,000	Interest income	$5,000
Loan – Mr Green	$100,000	Deposit – Mr Green	$95,000
		Interest charged and paid	

By comparing the two balance sheets, we see only a minor difference on the asset side. The real difference is on the liability side, where $5,000 has been transferred from the deposit account of Mr Green, to the Interest Income account of the commercial bank.

At this point, the quote by Professor Steve Keen bears repeating:

 The real story is the commercial banks generating money and making profit for themselves by creating debt.

Professor Steve Keen
Interviewed by Chris Martenson on 8 June 2012

Chapter 22 : Constraint on money creation

That is what our money system is. If there were no debts in our money system, there wouldn't be any money.

Mr Marriner Stoddard Eccles
Past Chairman of the Federal Reserve
1934 - 1948

With both the Deposit model and the Multiplier model of fractional reserve banking repudiated by monetary authorities, one may reasonably ask the question of whether there is any practical limit on the ability of commercial banks to create new digital money.

The public perception is that commercial banks can create new money at will and in unlimited quantities. However, this is not the case. To understand the constraints that exist, one merely has to examine what occurs when commercial banks create new money (i.e. when they monetise a debt) and also what occurs thereafter.

For example; the process of debt monetisation requires the participation of an external party to borrow money from the commercial bank. It is only when the party agrees to repay the money (with interest) that the bank proceeds with the transaction and deposits new money into their account. Consequently, debt monetisation is dependent on an outside party going into debt.

The major factors that slow money creation are:

- Willingness to shoulder debt.
- Currency note withdrawals.
- Transfer of deposits.
- Bank insolvency.
- Basel accords.

Willingness to shoulder debt

The most obvious constraint on money creation is evident from the term **debt monetisation**; since commercial banks can only create new money if someone (e.g. a person, a corporation, a government) is willing to enter into an agreement to borrow money from the bank, and thereby shoulder the obligation to repay the debt with interest.

The fear of bankruptcy is a natural and necessary emotion that inhibits rational people from entering into risky financial arrangements. Unfortunately, governments have less restraint, and readily pass their burden of debt onto the public, including future generations.

Shifting an obligation into the future is reminiscent of the successful advertising campaigns run by airlines; with their slogan of Fly Now, Pay Later. The more acquiescent the public is to repaying future debt, the more money is created by the commercial banks. Conversely, the more reluctant the public is to shouldering future debt, the less new money is created by the commercial banks.

Target cash ratio

The amount of currency (i.e. notes and coins) that commercial banks need to hold at their branches and in their ATMs is proportional to the amount of deposits that they have on their balance sheet. This relationship is sometimes referred to as the **target cash ratio**, and is defined as follows:

$$\text{Target cash ratio} = \frac{\text{Notes and coins}}{\text{Deposits}}$$

This ratio is not related to the amount of central bank money that commercial banks hold in reserve accounts at the central bank. The target cash ratio is used by the commercial banks to estimate the amount of physical currency that they should hold.

Bank runs

If the public lose confidence in a commercial bank, a bank run can ensue as depositors attempt to withdraw their money in the form of physical currency. A bank run occurred in 2007 at Northern Rock in Britain. This was the first bank run in Britain since 1866, and at the time Northern Rock was the country's fifth-biggest mortgage lender.

During a bank run, the target cash ratio (used to estimate the stock of physical currency) becomes irrelevant, as the number of depositors wanting to withdraw their money in the form of cash overwhelms the system and lays waste prior plans.

Buying currency notes

To examine the impact of a significant increase in the demand for physical currency, assume that a commercial bank has a simplified balance sheet as below. On the credit side of the balance sheet is $800 of deposits that could potentially be converted into currency notes.

Commercial Bank – Balance Sheet			
Assets		Liabilities	
Cash at RBA	$100	Equity	$200
Loans	$900	Deposits	$800
Insufficient cash			

When a commercial bank buys currency notes from the central bank, they pay with central bank money. In our example, the commercial bank only has $100 of central bank money. Consequently, it can only purchase $100 of currency notes. If the demand for physical currency surges, the commercial bank will encounter problems. To obtain additional central bank money, the commercial bank does either or both of the following:

- Borrow central bank money from other commercial banks.
- Borrow central bank money from the central bank.

Borrow from other banks

To elucidate a point, the following exaggerated scenario is used. Assume depositors want to withdraw all their deposits in the form of currency notes. To meet the demand the commercial bank must have $800 of central bank money. To reach this level, the commercial bank borrows $700 from Bank A. The commercial bank balance sheet now looks as follows:

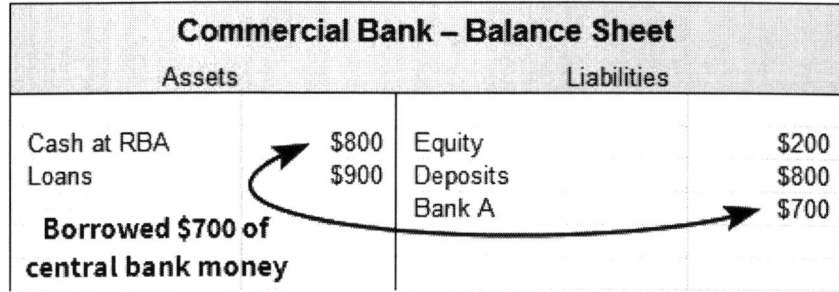

Commercial Bank – Balance Sheet			
Assets		Liabilities	
Cash at RBA	$800	Equity	$200
Loans	$900	Deposits	$800
		Bank A	$700
Borrowed $700 of central bank money			

The commercial bank is in a position to buy the currency notes and pays the central bank $800. Once the depositors withdraw their money (in the form of notes) the commercial bank balance sheet looks as follows:

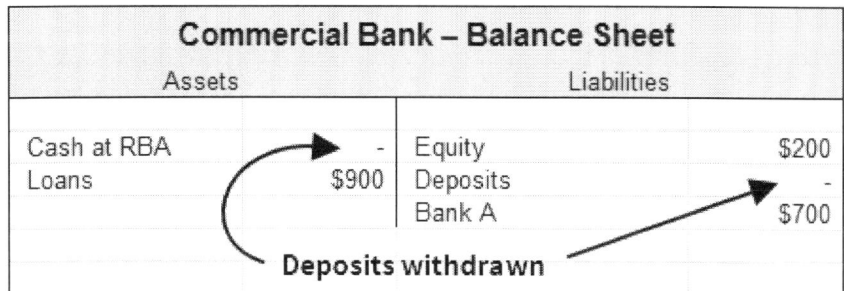

The result is the commercial bank replacing one liability (i.e. Deposits) with another, i.e. Bank A. Inter-bank transactions are only possible if commercial banks are willing to lend central bank money to each other. The global financial crisis of 2008 started when banks became reluctant to lend to other banks.

Commercial banks strive to keep their account balances at the central bank as low as possible. Commercial banks that have excess liquidity (i.e. surplus central bank money) only lend such money if the borrowing banks are sufficiently trusted to repay the amount with interest.

Borrow from central bank

Again, an exaggerated scenario is used. Assume the commercial bank approaches the central bank in order to borrow central bank money. To enter into a repurchase agreement with the central bank, the commercial bank must have government bonds. To obtain the bonds, it does the following:

- Sells $700 of assets (i.e. loans).
- Buys $700 of government bonds.

Once the commercial bank has $800 of central bank money, its balance sheet looks as follows:

Commercial Bank – Balance Sheet		
Assets	**Liabilities**	
Cash at RBA $800	Equity	$200
Loans $200	Deposits	$800
Sold assets and bought bonds to obtain central bank money.		

The commercial bank buys the currency notes and pays the central bank $800. Once the depositors withdraw their money (in the form of notes) the commercial bank balance sheet looks as follows:

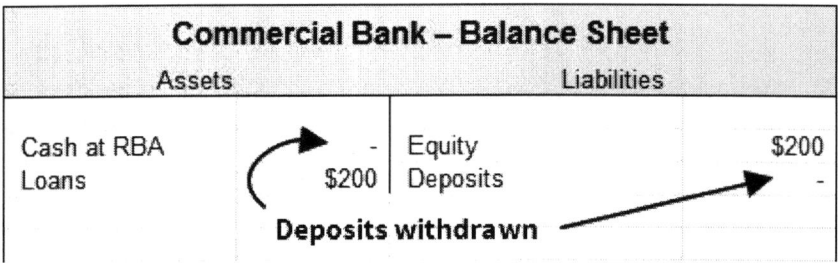

Commercial Bank – Balance Sheet		
Assets	**Liabilities**	
Cash at RBA -	Equity	$200
Loans $200	Deposits	-
Deposits withdrawn		

The end result is the destruction of the commercial bank balance sheet, since it is left with only $200 of loans to generate interest income. Consequently, commercial banks strive to limit borrowing from the central bank. Two additional reasons why commercial banks avoid the route of selling assets are:

- It becomes newsworthy very quickly - leading to a collapse in the bank share price.
- It drives the price of the asset down – leading to a "fire sale" condition.

Liquidity risk

While currency notes are still used throughout the economy, commercial banks will be cautious about unbridled money creation. Commercial banks do not want to run out of central bank money, or out of the ability to borrow central bank money, since they need it to purchase currency notes. The risk  of being unable to obtain central bank money is called liquidity risk.

Transfer deposits

When depositors transfer their account balance from one commercial bank to another, the process that is followed is essentially the same as outlined above – except that the recipient bank will obtain both the deposit (a liability) and central bank money (an asset).

Digital transfers are a concern to commercial banks due to the following:

- Transfers take very little effort.
- Transfers are generally for much larger amounts.

Consequently, commercial banks monitor the growth of their balance sheet (via debt monetisation) and the levels of their deposits very carefully. Large and unexpected transfers can lead to a liquidity crisis.

Bank solvency

Bank solvency is defined as the ability to pay a debt or a liability.

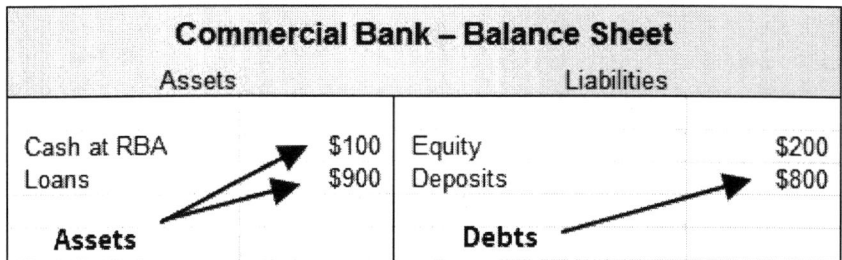

In our example, the assets of the bank exceed the debt by $200 – which is reflected in the value of the equity. During the global financial crisis many banks found the value of their assets to be significantly lower than reported.

If we devalue the assets by $300, then the equity of the bank becomes negative – meaning the bank is insolvent.

Commercial Bank – Balance Sheet			
Assets		Liabilities	
Cash at RBA	$100	*Equity*	*-$100*
Loans	$600	Deposits	$800
	$700		$700
Devalued			

Commercial banks must ensure they have sufficient equity to endure economic downturns where assets are devalued. They also need to increase equity as the bank monetises debt and records new loans in its balance sheet. If equity is too small, they run the risk of becoming insolvent.

Basel Accords

The question of how much equity a commercial bank should have relative to its assets is answered by the Basel Accords. The accords are a set of recommendations issued by the Basel Committee on Banking Supervision which meets at the Bank for International Settlements in Basel, Switzerland.

The accords are not legally binding on countries, but most have passed a version thereof into law in the form of banking regulations. To date three different accords have been issued:

- Basel 1 (introduced in 1988)
- Basel 2 (introduced in 2004)
- Basel 3 (introduced in 2010)

The accords are not static, given their subsequent updates and their delayed implementations. Basel 3 is re-scheduled for implementation in March 2019. The accords address the three pillars of Basel, namely:

The pillar of interest is Minimum Capital Requirements (known as the capital adequacy rule). The pillar provides a guideline to banks when they calculate their optimal level of equity.

Returning to our example; the capital adequacy rule provides a guideline of the amount of equity required (on the liability side) relative to the amount of assets in the balance sheet.

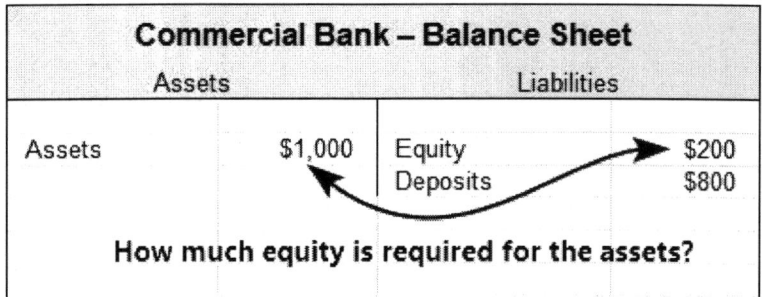

Capital adequacy does not look at the deposits of the bank, but only at the assets. Below is a simplified explanation of the process. The first step is to calculate the risk weighted assets, as opposed to the reported assets.

One: Risk weighted assets

This step has three components:

- Rank assets by risk.
- Assign a weighting of 0%, 10%, 20%, 50% or 100% to each asset.
- Sum the risk weighted values.

Assets that are high risk (e.g. commercial loans) should have a high risk weighting (i.e. 100%), while assets that are low risk (e.g. cash) should have a low risk weighting (i.e. 0%).

The Reserve Bank of New Zealand published a document entitled "Capital adequacy ratios for banks – simplified explanation and example of calculation", where they provide a framework to calculate risk weighted assets. The framework uses the categories of cash, government bonds, lending to banks, mortgages, commercial loans and fixed assets. Using this framework, we divide the $1,000 of assets into the categories.

Assets	Risk	Value	Risk weighted
Cash	0%	$50	$0
Govt Bonds	10%	$50	$5
Lending to banks	20%	$50	$10
Home loans	50%	$600	$300
Commercial loans	100%	$200	$200
Fixed assets	100%	$50	$50
		$1,000	$565

The Risk weighted column is the result of multiplying the two previous columns. What the framework does is take the asset value of $1,000 and adjust it lower – and declare that $565 is the real value that the bank can lose in a time of financial crisis.

Two: Capital adequacy ratio

The second step is to calculate the capital adequacy ratio of the bank. This ratio is then compared to the number provided by Basel. We calculate the capital adequacy ratio from the numbers above:

$$35\% \text{ (capital adequacy ratio)} = \frac{\$200 \text{ (actual capital)}}{\$565 \text{ (risk weighted assets)}}$$

Our capital adequacy ratio is 35%. Basel recommends that this number never be less than 8%. This means that the bank is sufficiently capitalised.

Another way of using the formula is to calculate the minimum equity that the bank needs (according to Basel). We switch the formula around and enter 8%. The result is below:

$$\$45.20 \text{ (minimum capital)} = 8\% \text{ x } \$565 \text{ (risk weighted assets)}$$

This says we only need $45.20 of equity to meet the Basel standard.

Slow down

Debt monetisation is not totally without limits. The constraints discussed are not absolute in the sense that a line exists that cannot be crossed. Rather, the constraints act as a mechanism to slow commercial banks in their headlong rush to monetise more debt and maximize profit.

The resolution to this issue rests not in better regulations, but rather in the concept of Fair Money, as set out in subsequent chapters.

Chapter 23 :   Consequences

There are two ways to conquer and enslave a country.
One is by the sword. The other is by debt.

John Adams
Second president of the United States
1797 – 1801

We examine the consequence of debt monetisation, and the effect our debt-based monetary system has on our lives.

Perpetual debt

When a debt is monetised, the value of the debt (i.e. the loan) is equal to the value of the new deposit. As time passes, interest accrues on the debt and the value of the debt becomes greater than the value of the deposit. For example; once 5% of interest as added to a loan, the situation is as follows:

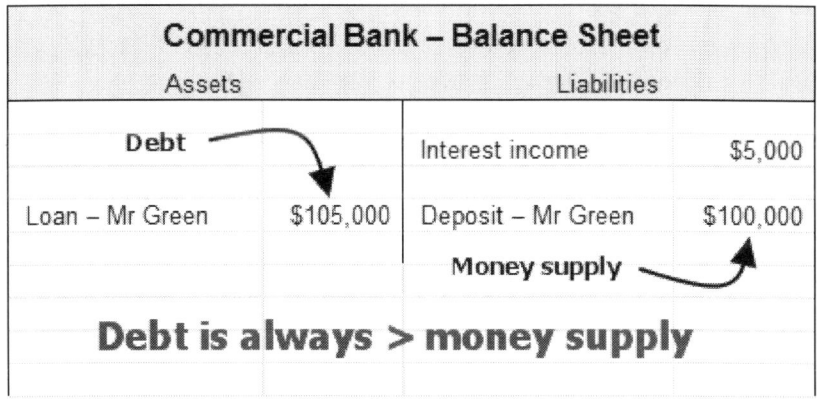

This scenario is germane to each loan advanced by commercial banks. It follows that the aggregate of all loans is greater than the aggregate of all deposits. This is perpetual debt, and perpetual debt is slavery.

The Fair Money solution will eliminate perpetual debt.

Devalued currency

Monetary inflation is an increase in the quantity of money. Price inflation is a general increase in prices. Wikipedia states:

> There is general agreement among economists that there is a causal relationship between monetary inflation and price inflation.

Examining price inflation as a sequence of annual price increases is interesting, but it is more instructive to examine price inflation as a reduction in the purchasing power of the Australian dollar.

 Lenin is said to have declared that the best way to destroy the capitalist system was to debauch the currency. By a continuing process of **inflation**, governments can **confiscate, secretly and unobserved**, an important part of the wealth of their citizens.

John Maynard Keynes

Since March 1960, the Australian dollar has lost 93% of its purchasing power. One of the statutory objectives of the Reserve Bank is:

> The **stability** of the currency of Australia.

Dictionary.com defines stability as: continuance without change. One can hardly consider the plunging value of the Australian dollar as being without change.

The Fair Money solution will stabilise the value of the Australian dollar.

A rigged market

There is a strong relationship between the target cash rate (as set by the Reserve Bank of Australia), and the variable rate that commercial banks charge on their loans.

The Reserve Bank states on its web site:

> Monetary policy decisions involve **setting the interest rate on overnight loans** in the money market. **Other interest rates in the economy are influenced by this interest rate** to varying degrees...

Interest rates in the economy are not determined in the open market by forces of supply and demand – they are set by the central bank. The correlation between the target cash rate and the variable rate on commercial bank loans is evident in the graph below.

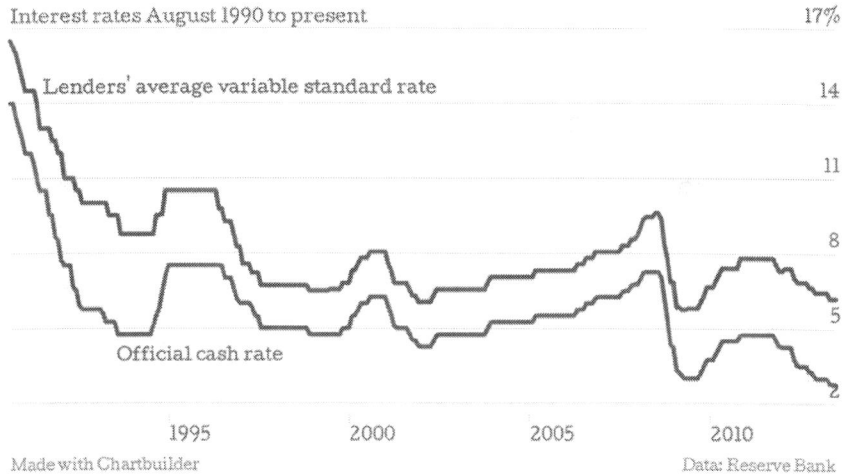

Interest rates August 1990 to present

Lenders' average variable standard rate

Official cash rate

17%

14

11

8

5

2

1995   2000   2005   2010

Made with Chartbuilder   Data: Reserve Bank

The Fair Money solution will remove such market manipulation.

Bail-ins

In 2012 the International Monetary Fund published a document entitled From Bail-out to Bail-in: Mandatory Debt Restructuring of Systemic Financial Institutions. The document defines a bail-in as below:

> Bail-in ... is a statutory power of a resolution authority ... to restructure the **liabilities** [i.e. the deposits] of a distressed financial institution by writing down its **unsecured debt** [i.e. its obligation to re-pay depositors] and/or converting it [i.e. the deposits] to equity.

Recall that in the books of a commercial bank, a deposit is both a liability and an unsecured debt. The extract says that when a commercial bank becomes financially distressed, deposits will either be **reduced** (i.e. confiscated) or **converted into shares**.

Bank bail-ins is a reality of life. Numerous articles are published on the subject, including details of the first major casualty in Europe, namely the Bank of Cyprus. Depositors with more than €100,000 in their deposit accounts had 47.5% of their funds confiscated.

The Bank of Cyprus was the first high profile incident, and it will definitely not be the last.

The Fair Money solution eliminates the possibility of bail-ins.

Business cycles

Two powerful economic forces are set in motion when a bank monetises a debt. These two forces are:

- Monetary inflation in the short term – as new money is created and spent into circulation. Pressure exists for prices to rise.
- Monetary deflation in the medium and longer term – as loans are repaid and existing money is destroyed. Pressure exists for prices to fall.

Diagrammatically the forces work as follows:

Economic forces released by Debt Monetisation

Prices

Debt repayments

Monetary
inflation

Time in years

When these forces are aggregated from multiple occurrences of debt monetisation (i.e. from thousands of mortgages), the economy contorts in artificial spasms of monetary expansion and contraction, more commonly referred to as boom and bust cycles.

The Fair Money solution will dampen these business cycles.

Diminishing returns

Borrowing money to fund an enterprise only makes economic sense if each dollar that is borrowed generates a positive return. Since commercial bank money exists only by virtue of having being borrowed, an economy can only grow if each dollar of debt (or money) contributes positively to GDP. In the USA, the return on borrowed money has been on a downward trajectory since 1960, and became negative in 2008. Quantitative easing followed shortly thereafter.

Getting Less and Less in Return

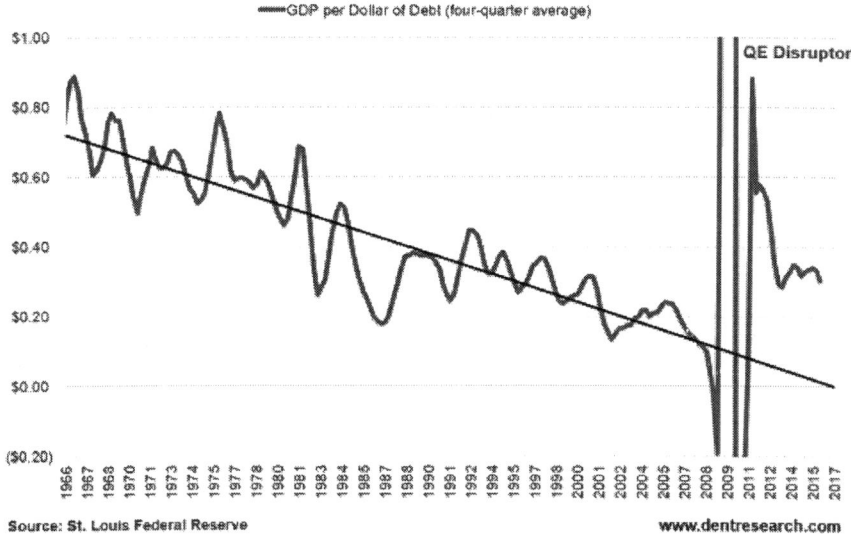

Source: St. Louis Federal Reserve   www.dentresearch.com

The data in the graph is sourced from the St. Louis Federal Reserve. Entry into negative territory signals the terminal phase of the monetary experiment called debt monetisation. The quantitative easing programs undertaken by the Federal Reserve spiked the figures temporarily; only to have them resume their downward trajectory. This indicates the ineffectual nature of QE.

The Fair Money solution will reduce debt and increase GDP.

Complexity

The quote from John Kenneth Galbraith bears repeating:

> The study of money, above all other fields in economics, is one in which complexity is used to disguise truth or to evade truth, not to reveal it.

Our monetary system is portrayed as being immensely complex, with terms such as fractional reserve ratio, intermediation, money multiplier etc. used to explain how it works. The real insult to the public is that these terms are irrelevant and have no practical application in modern banking. Our monetary system is cloaked in misleading jargon, pontificated upon by uninformed commentators and legislated by ignorant politicians.

The Fair Money solution provides transparency and simplicity.

Sale of public assets

Governments around the world are responding to budget deficits with the sale of public assets, such as ports, highways, electricity grids, telecommunication grids, water treatment plants etc. In each case, politicians pontificate about the need to raise revenue, and the need to introduce competition into the market. At each turn, lower consumer prices are touted.

Empirical evidence shows that following privatisation programs, the cost of utilities (e.g. water or electricity bills) rise dramatically.

A single example will suffice: The State Electricity Commission of Victoria was created in 1921, and provided cheap electricity to the state for a period of 70 years. Following an election in 1992, the State Electricity Commission was sold and today the public continues to shoulder the cost of this decision. An Associate Editor of The Age newspaper stated:

> Bill shock doesn't quite describe the experience, for we have become hardened to the ridiculous amounts being charged for what is an essential service.

The Fair Money solution will reduce the budgetary need to sell public assets.

Malinvestment

Commercial banks are driven to generate profit for their shareholders. They operate without the social conscience that is inalienable to human beings, and which guides our conduct regarding the environment and other people. As human beings we stop to assist a grandmother who has stumbled and fallen, we pick up trash that has been left in our parks and we give a dollar to the musician busking on the corner.

Banks do not have an obligation to promote the public good.

Alexander Dielius
CEO Goldman Sachs (Germany, Austria, Eastern Europe)
January 2010

Commercial banks are more likely to provide funds to industries that generate high returns and have low risk (such as casinos) than to public enterprises that are unprofitable (such as a library). No account is taken of the fact that public enterprises shape our culture and the environment in which children are raised.

The Fair Money solution will remedy the misallocation of investments.

Alice in Wonderland

When a member of the public states that they have "money in the bank" they assume that they have deposited something of value, and that the bank will record:

- Their deposit as an asset, and
- The obligation of the bank to return their money as a liability.

Commercial banking worked this way when gold and silver coins were used as money. This banking model was abandoned decades ago, and yet it still lingers in the deep recess of the public mind.

Prior chapters have set out in detail that when commercial banks lend money (i.e. when they monetise a debt), they simultaneously create:

- A deposit - which the public considers to be money.
- A loan - which is the obligation of the borrower to repay the money.

Readers are encouraged to stop for a minute and contemplate the circular reasoning that underpins our debt-based monetary system. A prompt is provided in the diagram below:

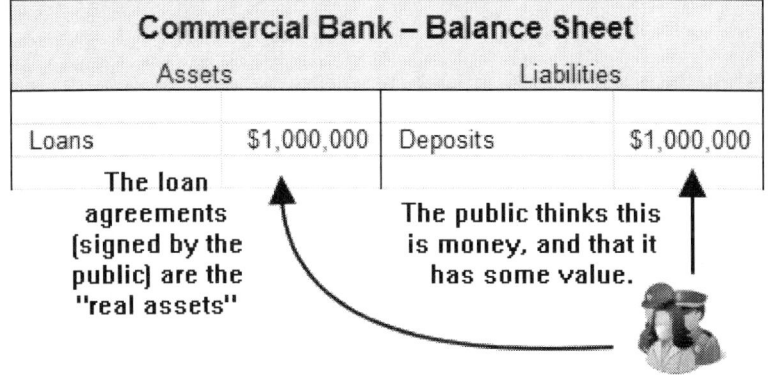

Commercial Bank – Balance Sheet

Assets		Liabilities	
Loans	$1,000,000	Deposits	$1,000,000

The loan agreements (signed by the public) are the "real assets"

The public thinks this is money, and that it has some value.

The diagram above provides a snapshot of our current situation, which is that:

- The public believe that deposits have value.
- The value of the deposits is determined by the value of the loans.
- The value of the loans is determined by the ability of the public to repay their debt.

And there you have the circular argument. Looking at the reasoning in reverse; the ability of the public to repay their debt determines the value of the loans, and the value of the loans determines the value of the deposits.

Consequently, if the public ever tried to determine what it is that instils value into their deposits, they would end up staring into a mirror. This epiphany is uncomfortable and bewildering for many.

This circular reasoning is equivalent to the term "literary nonsense" used to describe Alice in Wonderland. Wikipedia defines a literary nonsense to be:

> Literary nonsense is a broad categorization of literature that balances elements that make sense with some that do not, with the effect of **subverting** language conventions or **logical reasoning**.

Our current monetary system is a monetary nonsense. The Fair Money solution will remove our monetary system from this world of absurdity and make believe.

Chapter 24 :   Fair Money solution

The banks should be limited in their lending power to the amount deposited by their clients while the issue of newer credits should be the function of public authority.

Archbishop of Canterbury
1942

Principles

Our current monetary system and that of the Fair Money solution are based on entirely different principles. The essence of each is given below:

Current monetary system:

> Commercial bank money exists only by virtue of being borrowed into circulation.

Fair Money solution:

> The national currency in all its forms (i.e. notes, coins and digital), should be created by an independent body and then spent into circulation by the government on public infrastructure. This independent body should measure and control the quantity of money in circulation, so that price inflation remains at zero.

New rules

The Fair Money solution requires an independent monetary authority, and a change in the role of commercial banks. Below is a summary of the proposed rules:

The independent monetary authority should:

- Create the national currency in all its forms.
- Place newly created money at the disposal of government.
- Ensure such money is spent on public infrastructure.
- Measure both monetary inflation and price inflation.
- Control the quantity of the national currency so that price inflation tends towards zero (i.e. maintain the value of the national currency).

The commercial banks should:

- Not create money in any way.
- Separate their assets from those of their clients.
- Create new legal structures to act as intermediaries between lenders and borrowers.

The Reserve Bank of Australia is ideally placed to fulfil the role of the independent monetary authority, since it already has the necessary infrastructure and expertise to perform the activities listed above.

New money classes

The Fair Money solution utilises two money classes, namely:

1. The national currency.
2. Gold and silver.

Everyone uses the same money

The national currency includes notes, coins and digital money. This new class will be used by all parties, namely:

- Independent monetary authority.
- Commercial banks.
- The public.

Gold and silver will be a concurrent currency, and provide to the public the freedom to select their preferred medium of exchange and their preferred store of value. This money class will act as a barometer, since major fluctuations in the price of gold and silver indicate that the national currency is mismanaged.

Superannuation funds

Superannuation funds in Australia operate as trusts. Superannuation funds are basically retirement or pension funds. Legislation sets minimum standards for these funds. Most funds publish their trust deeds and their annual reports online. A common definition of a trust is given below:

> An arrangement whereby a person (a trustee) holds property as its nominal owner for the good of one or more beneficiaries.

Superannuation funds have operated effectively for decades to manage the retirement money of millions of Australians. As at June 2015, Australians had over $2 trillion of assets in their superannuation funds.

Currency funds

The Fair Money solution proposes that currency trust funds be used to manage the $1.83 trillion of deposits held by Australians in commercial banks (as at September 2016). Commercial banks are steeped in the use of trust funds, and should be able to assume the role of trustee without any difficulty.

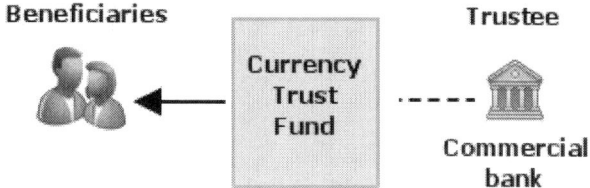

Legislation is required to create the legal framework in which the currency trust funds operate.

Accounting rules

There are differences between the balance sheet of commercial banks and those of legal trusts. For the purpose of explaining how the Fair Money solution works; the accounting approach used by commercial banks is retained. The objective is to convey an understanding of the Fair Money solution, even if the accounting entries and the reports presented fall short of the generally accepted accounting principles.

Backed by assets

Commercial bank money has no intrinsic value, and is not a claim on anything of tangible value. Historically, money did have intrinsic value. Below is a short list of countries where physical items passed as money:

- China and Ethiopia – blocks of salt.
- Mongolia and Serbia – bricks made from tea.
- Russia and Finland – animal furs.
- Solomon Islands – huge rounded stones.
- Italy – parmesan cheese.
- Chinese Zhou dynasty – knives inscribed with words.

The Fair Money solution is based on the notion that the national currency should be based on tangible assets, and that the assets should be:

- Publically owned.
- Productive.

For this reason the Fair Money solution states that new money must be **spent into circulation on public infrastructure**, in lieu of taxes.

Deposit is an asset

Commercial banks record client deposits as liabilities. Superannuation funds record the assets of their members (be it cash, shares or physical assets) to be just that, i.e. assets. The Fair Money solution follows this approach, since it is intuitive and the most appropriate for recording the assets of depositors. This means that currency trust funds will record deposits as follows:

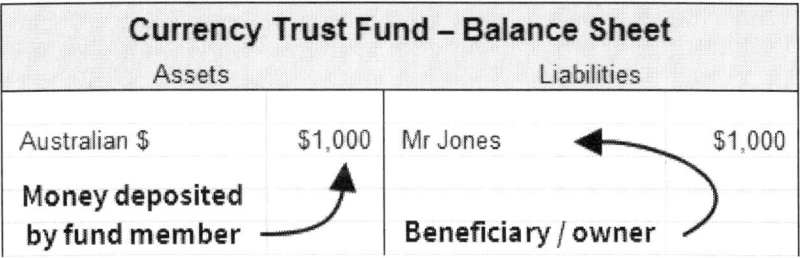

Currency Trust Fund – Balance Sheet			
Assets		Liabilities	
Australian $	$1,000	Mr Jones	$1,000
Money deposited by fund member		Beneficiary / owner	

Currency account types

The Fair Money solution proposes the following type of accounts at each currency trust fund:

Savings: This is a non-lending account, in that deposits into the account will not be lent to another party. Since no lending occurs, no interest is earned. Money in this account is effectively removed from circulation.

Current: This is a transmission account, in that the account is used to facilitate payments and to receive money from other parties. Since no lending occurs, no interest is earned. Money in this account is effectively removed from circulation.

Investment: This is a lending account, in that money deposited into the account is available for lending to other parties. Interest will be earned, and the interest rate will be based on supply and demand.

Same statements

Client account statements will be no different from those issued by commercial banks. For example, a statement issued by a currency trust fund would look as follows:

Mr Green – Current account statement				
Date	Description	Deposit	Withdrawl	Balance
03 Jan	Wage	$1,200		$1,200
12 Jan	Food		$100	$1,100
20 Jan	Rent		$250	$850
25 Jan	Clothes		$95	$755
02 Feb	Wage	$1,200		$1,955
19 Feb	Movies		$45	$1,910
20 Feb	Food		$65	$1,845

Investment pools

Many superannuation funds provide investment pools into which retirement funds can be deposited. Below is an example of three investment pools at an existing superannuation fund:

Investment Option	Since inception (% p.a.)**	10-year (% p.a.)**	7-year (% p.a.)**	5-year (% p.a.)**
Ready-Made Investment Pools				
Conservative Pool (1/7/95*)	6.61	5.73	5.53	7.08
Core Pool (1/8/87*)	**8.90**	**6.88**	**6.36**	**9.78**
Shares Plus (1/7/95*)	8.61	7.33	7.11	10.74

Investment pools are similar to the investment accounts proposed in the Fair Money solution. Depositors who want to earn interest will transfer their money into such investment accounts/pools.

Earning interest

For example, if three depositors transferred their money into a Mining Investment Pool, then that investment account will look as follows:

Mining Investment Pool account			
Assets		Liabilities	
Australian $	$500,000	Mr Green	$200,000
		Mrs Purple	$100,000
		Mr Jones	$200,000

The trustees will follow the rules of the investment pool and decide how much money to lend and to whom. For example, the rules may require a cash buffer of 10% with the balance lent to companies in the mining industry. The investment pool may end up as follows:

Mining Investment Pool account			
Assets		Liabilities	
Australian $	$50,000	Mr Green	$200,000
BHP Billiton	$150,000	Mrs Purple	$100,000
Newmont	$300,000	Mr Jones	$200,000

In this example, the investment account lends a total of $450,000 to BHP Billiton and Newmont, while the three investors share equally in the risk and reward. Different investment accounts will pay different interest rates depending on risk and the supply and demand of money. This is monetary democracy at work.

Borrow money

Newmont will have two accounts, similar to any borrower that obtains a loan from a commercial bank. In this case $300,000 will be deposited into the Newmont current account, while the obligation to repay the loan is recorded in the Newmont loan account.

When interest is charged, the Mining Investment Pool account will increase its assets by the interest amount, while the Newmont loan account will be increased by the same amount.

New money

The Fair Money solution does not make a distinction between central bank money and commercial bank money. All participants in the economy will use the national currency as created by the independent monetary authority.

Money that is created will be deposited into a current account at a currency trust fund, where the trustee is the independent monetary authority, and the account holder is the government. The Reserve Bank of Australia is expected to fulfil the role of the independent monetary authority due to its existing infrastructure and experience.

RBA currency trust fund

The currency trust fund operated by the independent monetary authority should be run along the lines discussed above, except for the following:

- The fund will have one client – the Australian government.
- The fund is the only one where new money is deposited.

Commercial banks will no longer be allowed to create money in any form. As commercial bank clients repay their loans, the bank will demonetise the debt, thereby destroying commercial bank money.

The government will operate this account in the same manner it operates existing bank accounts. The only difference is that money created and deposited into this account can only be spent on public infrastructure.

The public infrastructure that is financed must be owned by the government or registered in a public trust, where the residents of Australia are the beneficiaries of the public trust.

Money that the government receives via taxation will continue to be spent on items such as defence, education, medical assistance etc.

By way of example; assume the independent monetary authority creates $1 million and deposits the money into the government current account. The transaction is recorded as follows:

RBA Currency Trust Fund – Balance sheet			
Assets		Liabilities	
Australian $	$1,000,000	Aus Government	$1,000,000
Newly created money		**Spend this on infrastructure**	

As the government spends the money on infrastructure projects, its current account will look as follows:

Government - Current account statement				
Date	Description	Deposit	Withdrawl	Balance
01 Jan	Seigniorage	$1,000,000		$1,000,000
12 Jan	Building project A		$250,000	$750,000
20 Jan	Building project B		$750,000	-

National Currency Account

The National Currency Account is the keystone in the operation of the Fair Money solution. The account will exist at the national level, and only one such account is required.

The National Currency Account will be maintained by the independent monetary authority and will record the following:

- Money held in all currency trust funds.
- Movement of money between currency trust funds.
- Public infrastructure financed.

In diagrammatic form, the relationship between the National Currency Account and the various currency trust funds is as follows:

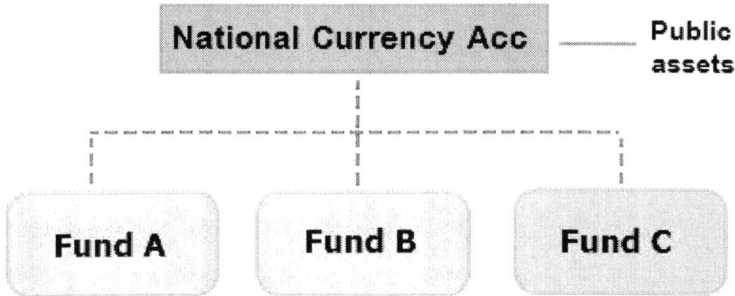

Function

When the independent monetary authority creates $1 million and deposits the money into the RBA Currency Trust Fund, the National Currency Account will look as follows:

National Currency Account			
Assets		Liabilities	
Australian $	$1,000,000	RBA Curr Trust Fund	$1,000,000

As money is transferred from one currency trust fund to another, the National Currency Account is updated. Assume that the government pays for two building projects, as shown in its current account statement above. The National Currency Account is updated to look as follows:

National Currency Account			
Assets		Liabilities	
Australian $	$1,000,000	RBA Curr Trust Fund	-
		Currency Trust Fund A	$250,000
		Currency Trust Fund B	$750,000

As the government itemises the public infrastructure that has been financed, the National Currency Account is updated to look as follows:

National Currency Account			
Assets		Liabilities	
Australian $	-	RBA Curr Trust Fund	-
School	$250,000	Currency Trust Fund A	$250,000
Hospital	$750,000	Currency Trust Fund B	$750,000

The National Currency Account provides the following information:

- The national currency is backed by two public assets.
- $1 million is deposited at two currency trust funds.

In a nutshell, the National Currency Account records the physical assets that underpin the national currency and the movement of the national currency between various currency trust funds. The National Currency Account is necessary for the operation of an asset-based currency.

Inter-fund payments

In our current monetary system, Exchange Settlement accounts are used to facilitate inter-bank payments. Under the Fair Money solution, the National Currency Account will perform a similar function when money is transferred from one currency trust fund to another.

As mentioned in the chapter on Exchange Settlement accounts, inter-bank payments are comprised of three separate but related transactions. This situation remains unchanged with the use of the National Currency Account.

Below is a diagram that provides a high-level view of how inter-fund payments are executed. An example of how the National Currency Account works is provided thereafter.

Independent Monetary Authority

National Currency Account	
Currency Trust Fund A	- $1,000
Currency Trust Fund B	+ $1,000

National currency

Mr Green
- $1,000

Mrs Purple
+ $1,000

One: Payer fund

Assume Mr Green has $10,000 in an account at Currency Trust Fund A. Mr Green makes a payment of $1,000 to Mrs Purple who has an account at Currency Trust Fund B. Prior to the payment the balance sheet of the Currency Trust Fund A looks as follows:

Currency Trust Fund A – Balance Sheet			
Assets		Liabilities	
Australian $	$10,000	Mr Green	$10,000

The administrators deduct $1,000 from the account of Mr Green and decrease the assets by a similar amount. The balance sheet of the fund now looks as follows:

184 | Fair Money

Currency Trust Fund A – Balance Sheet			
Assets		**Liabilities**	
Australian $	$9,000	Mr Green	$9,000

The administrators send a message to the independent monetary authority with details of the inter-fund payment.

Two: Independent monetary authority

Prior to the payment, the National Currency Account looks as follows:

National Currency Account			
Assets		**Liabilities**	
Assets	$30,000	Currency Trust Fund A	$10,000
		Currency Trust Fund B	$20,000

Once the message is received, independent monetary authority transfers $1,000 from Currency Trust Fund A to Currency Trust Fund B.

National Currency Account			
Assets		**Liabilities**	
Assets	$30,000	Currency Trust Fund A	$9,000
		Currency Trust Fund B	$21,000

The independent monetary authority sends a message to Currency Trust Fund B with instructions to credit the account of Mrs Purple with $1,000.

Three: Receiving fund

Prior to the payment, the balance sheet of Currency Trust Fund B looks as follows:

Currency Trust Fund B – Balance Sheet			
Assets		Liabilities	
Australian $	$20,000	Mrs Purple	-
		Other depositors	$20,000

Once the message is received, the administrators credit the account of Mrs Purple with $1,000 and increase the assets by a similar amount.

Currency Trust Fund B – Balance Sheet			
Assets		Liabilities	
Australian $	$21,000	Mrs Purple	$1,000
		Other depositors	$20,000

Inter-fund payments under the Fair Money solution follow the same steps as inter-bank payments under our current monetary system.

Directed investments

Political parties come and go, and while in power they are swayed by both public trends and special interest groups. If the national currency is backed by productive public assets, then some discretion should be given to the independent monetary authority to determine the nature and quality of such public assets.

Recall that one of the statutory objectives of the central bank is to:

> Contribute to the economic prosperity and welfare of the people of Australia.

To this end it is not unreasonable to authorise the independent monetary authority to direct a portion of newly created money to specific public investments to enhance the prosperity and welfare of Australians.

Short term lending

There is a scenario where it is beneficial for the independent monetary authority to create and invest money into short-term lending pools. The scenario is:

- Where the government receives money for infrastructure, but can only spend that money in the future. For example, the government receives $200 million for a new bridge, but can only pay the bulk of the money once the bridge is complete. This means that the money is sitting idle and not circulating in the economy.

SHORT TERM PARKING ONLY

Short term lending provides temporary liquidity to the market. The repayments on the short term loans will be set to match the future payments of the government on their infrastructure projects. When a repayment is received, the independent monetary authority destroys the money. When the government pays for the bridge, the money supply in the economy is restored to its desired level.

The objective of short term lending is to add temporary liquidity; not to influence interest rates. Interest rates should be set by the market, and not by the government or any private entity.

Chapter 25 :   Fair Money benefits

The chief duty of the National Government in connection with the currency of the country is to coin money and declare its value... He who controls the money supply of a nation controls the nation.

James Garfield
19 November 1831 – 19 September 1881
20th President of the United States

Research reports

In 2012 the Research Department at the International Monetary Fund published a document entitled The Chicago Plan Revisited. The document lists the benefits that will accrue to a nation if it adopts a monetary system where money is created by the government, and not by the commercial banks. The benefits are:

- Dramatic reduction in public debt.
- Dramatic reduction in private debt.
- Increase in GDP of 10%.
- Price inflation dropping to zero.
- Smoother business cycles.
- No bank runs.

In 2010, Professor Kaoru Yamaguchi presented a paper entitled "On the Liquidation of Government Debt under a Debt-free Monetary System" to the 28th International Conference of the System Dynamics Society in South Korea. The paper lists the benefits that will accrue to a nation if it adopts a monetary system where the government issues all the money in circulation. The benefits are:

- Higher Gross Domestic Product.
- Elimination of government debt.

The paper also details the mathematical model used to reach these conclusions. Students on this subject are encouraged to find and read these documents, and to reach their own conclusion without the sway of the media.

Banking fears

The International Monetary Fund points out that the banking industry has very little to fear from the deployment of The Chicago Plan, when it states:

> **None of these benefits come at the expense of diminishing the core useful functions of a private financial system**... Private financial institutions would continue to play a key role in providing a state-of-the-art payments system, facilitating the efficient allocation of capital to its most productive uses...

List of benefits

Listed below are the section headings from a prior chapter which details the ruinous consequences of our current debt-based monetary system. These headings are used as prompts to highlight how the Fair Money solution addresses each topic.

Perpetual debt: With the Fair Money solution, newly created money will be spent into circulation rather than being lent into circulation. Both documents mentioned above point to a significant reduction in public debt if the government creates the money in circulation.

Devalued currency: With the Fair Money solution, the mandate of the independent monetary authority would be to measure and control the quantity of money in circulation, so that price inflation tends to zero.

Existing monetary policy in Australia has seen the dollar lose 93% of its value since 1960. Only by stating that price inflation should be zero, can one hope to achieve it.

Rigged market: Monetary policy is executed when the central bank sets the interest rate on central bank money. This is interest rate fixing – pure and simple. With the Fair Money solution, interest rates are not set by any person or entity, but by the forces of supply and demand. This is the free market at work.

Bails-ins: The Research Department at the International Monetary Fund has stated that under The Chicago Plan, bank runs will be completely eliminated.

Business cycles: Library shelves are replete with books on the recurring boom and bust cycles that decimate large segments of society, and transfer wealth from the many to the few. This is a natural consequence of our debt-based monetary system. Implementing The Chicago Plan will smooth out business cycles, and significantly reduce private and public debt.

Diminishing returns: Since 1960 each US dollar borrowed into existence has generated less than a dollar of gross domestic product. Implementing The Chicago Plan will increase gross domestic product by 10% without any increase in debt.

Complexity: The complexity of our current monetary system can be gauged by the numerous conflicting explanations of how it supposedly works. Most of these explanations are inaccurate. The Fair Money solution provides a simple explanation of how it works, free of the usual jargon.

Sale of public assets: With the Fair Money solution, new money will be spent into circulation on public infrastructure. This will terminate the need to sell public assets, which has occurred under the guise of lower prices and better service. Both are false and self-serving.

Malinvestment: With the Fair Money solution, depositors will select the investment pools where they want their money applied. This is monetary democracy at work.

Alice in Wonderland: With the Fair Money solution, the value of the national currency will be determined by the value of public infrastructure, and not by the aggregate debt of the population.

Population and productivity

There are additional factors that affect the level of prices in the economy. They are population growth and productivity.

If the population increases while the money supply remained constant, then the quantity of money relative to each person declines. This is relative monetary deflation, which invariably leads to falling prices. An increase in productivity also leads to lower prices, as more goods are manufactured per unit of input.

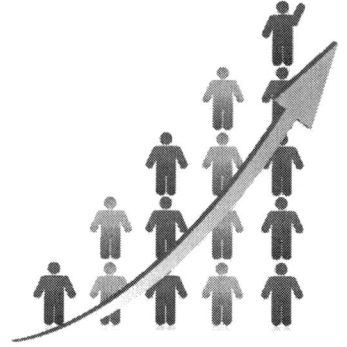

If population and productivity increase, then additional money should be created by the independent monetary authority to keep price inflation at zero. The numbers below are used to estimate the quantity of money that can be created and spent into circulation:

- 2015 population growth in Australia is 1.34% (World Bank).
- 2015 productivity in Australian is 2.8% (Productivity Commission).
- Commercial bank money in circulation in Australia as at September 2016 is $1.83 trillion.

Adding the two percentages together we get 4.14%. The percentage is applied to the figure of commercial bank money:

$$\$75 \text{ billion} = 4.1\% * \$1.83 \text{ trillion}$$

This means that $75 billion of money can be created by the independent monetary authority, as part of its mandate to keep price inflation at zero. If government expenditure is constant, then taxes can be cut by $75 billion.

Removed from circulation

Recall that under the Fair Money solution; when money is deposited into a savings account, such money is effectively withdrawn from circulation.

If the amount of money in all saving accounts is significant, then it can lead to price deflation - since the money is no longer circulating in the economy. This scenario can occur as the population ages and as their investment risk profile changes to that of being financially conservative.

In this case, the independent monetary authority is expected to create additional money that will be spent on public infrastructure. The objective is to keep the amount of money circulating in the economy constant. Even without the benefit of actual numbers, the end result will be lower taxes.

Summary

In a single line, the role of the independent monetary authority will be to:

Measure and control the quantity of the national currency in circulation, so that price inflation remains constant at zero.

Empirically, population growth, increased productivity and technological progress lead to gradual price reductions. With the target rate of price inflation set at zero, the independent monetary authority can counter gradual price reductions by increasing the quantity of money in circulation. The end result is:

- Spending on infrastructure.
- Reduced taxes.

Chapter 26 :   Transition to Fair Money

Until the control of the issue of currency and credit is restored to government and recognized as its most conspicuous and sacred responsibility, all talk of the sovereignty of Parliament and of democracy is idle and futile.

William Lyon Mackenzie King
Canadian Prime Minister
1935

Transition

A transition to a Fair Money system will not occur overnight. Similar to an overweight person; shedding unwanted kilograms takes months if not years. The good news is that traversing the path to debt emancipation is not difficult, and merely requires the will of good men and women.

Change to our monetary system must be affected at the national level, and this requires the involvement of federal government. The following legal frameworks need to be created:

- Legislation for the operation of currency trust funds.
- A charter for the independent monetary authority.
- New regulations for the banking industry.

Destroy and create

Commercial banks monetise new debts on a daily basis. This increases the money supply. Borrowers also repay their debts to commercial banks (if only in part) on a daily basis. This reduces the money supply. Once commercial banks are restrained from creating new money, debt monetisation will cease and only debt demonetisation will occur.

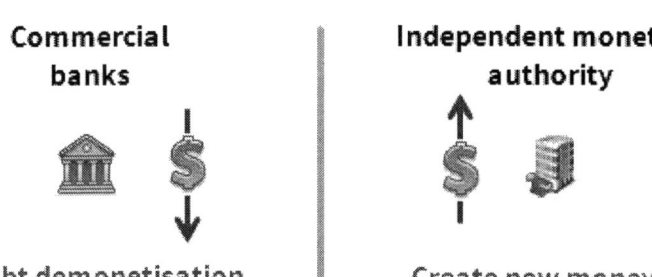

As loans are repaid and commercial banks destroy money, the independent monetary authority will create an equal amount of new money in order to keep the money supply constant. The money created will be placed at the disposal of government to be spent on public infrastructure, in lieu of taxes.

Separate bank & public assets

The public considers bank deposits to be their assets. Banks consider loans to be their assets.

A major objective of the transition is to **separate bank assets and public assets**. This is achieved by transferring all deposits to currency trust funds, while retaining loans at commercial banks.

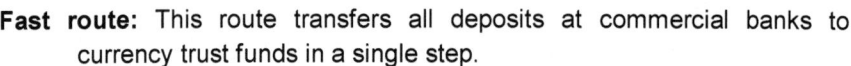

The transition has two possible routes; fast or slow.

Fast route: This route transfers all deposits at commercial banks to currency trust funds in a single step.

Slow route: This route retains deposits at commercial banks, and records the natural reduction in deposit balances as loans are repaid and money is destroyed.

Slow route: Demonetisation

To elucidate the slow route, a simplified bank balance sheet is presented. Note that the total money supply (i.e. deposits) is $1 million.

Commercial Bank – Balance Sheet			
Assets		Liabilities	
Loans	$1,000,000	Deposit - ABC	$850,000
		Deposit - Mr Green	$150,000

Assume Mr Green has a loan of $100,000 and a deposit of $150,000. Mr Green decides to repay his loan with the money in his deposit account. When the loan is repaid, debt demonetisation occurs. The bank balance sheet now looks as follows:

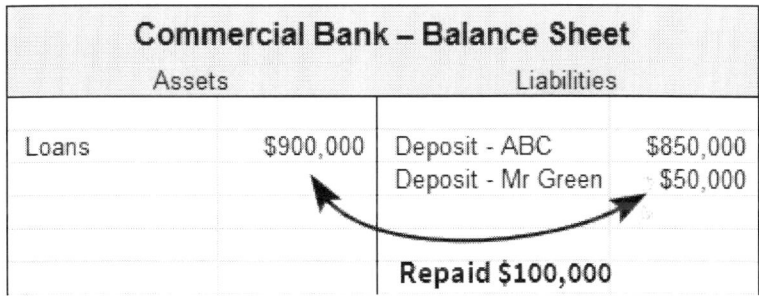

Commercial Bank – Balance Sheet			
Assets		Liabilities	
Loans	$900,000	Deposit - ABC	$850,000
		Deposit - Mr Green	$50,000
		Repaid $100,000	

At this point the money supply is reduced to $900,000.

Slow route: Money creation

The commercial bank informs the independent monetary authority that $100,000 of commercial bank money has been destroyed. The independent monetary authority creates $100,000 and deposits the money into an account at the RBA Currency Trust Fund. The government will now spend this money on public infrastructure.

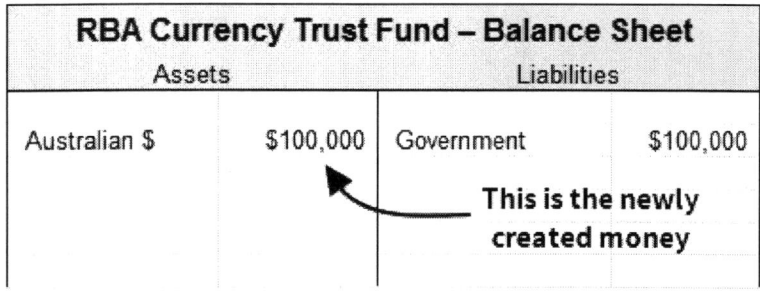

The money supply is now restored to $1 million. In a nutshell; when commercial bank loans are repaid, the money supply is reduced. The independent monetary authority responds by creating new money so that the total money supply in the economy remains constant, i.e. so that monetary inflation remains constant at zero.

Fast route: Move deposits

To elucidate the fast route, the same bank balance sheet is presented. Note that the total money supply (i.e. deposits) is $1 million.

Commercial Bank – Balance Sheet			
Assets		**Liabilities**	
Loans	$1,000,000	Deposit – ABC	$850,000
		Deposit – Mr Green	$150,000

The deposit accounts are transferred to a currency trust fund in a single step. To keep the balance sheet "balanced", the deposit entries are replaced with a single entry of $1 million as below:

Commercial Bank – Balance Sheet			
Assets		**Liabilities**	
Loans	$1,000,000	National Credit	$1,000,000

The entry is **National Credit**, and is discussed below. At the currency trust fund where the deposits are relocated, the balance sheet looks as follows:

Currency Trust Fund A – Balance Sheet			
Assets		Liabilities	
Australian $	$1,000,000	ABC	$850,000
		Mr Green	$150,000

National Credit

The reason for using the term **National Credit** is simple; it is the amount of seigniorage that the government never received when money was created by the commercial bank. The National Credit is a measure of the financial benefit owed to Australia and its residents.

The financial benefit (i.e. the seigniorage) is received when commercial bank loans are repaid, and the independent monetary authority creates new money (in order to keep the money supply constant). The new money will then be placed at the disposal of government to be spent on public infrastructure.

Fast route: Demonetisation

We examine what occurs when Mr Green repays his loan of $100,000. The first step occurs in the books of the currency trust fund as the money is paid to the commercial bank.

Currency Trust Fund A – Balance Sheet		
Assets	**Liabilities**	
Australian $ $1,000,000	ABC	$850,000
	Mr Green	$50,000
	Commercial Bank	$100,000
	Repay $100,000	

The loan being repaid was originally created via debt monetisation. As prior chapters have explained – when bank loans are repaid, money is destroyed. Consequently, the money used to repay the loan is removed from the balance sheet. The resulting balance sheet looks as follows:

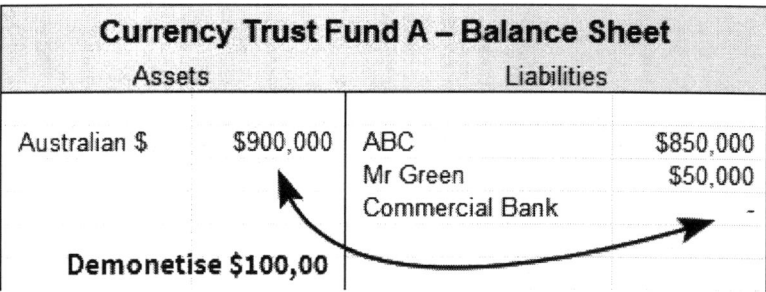

Currency Trust Fund A – Balance Sheet		
Assets	**Liabilities**	
Australian $ $900,000	ABC	$850,000
	Mr Green	$50,000
	Commercial Bank	-
Demonetise $100,00		

At this point the money supply is reduced to $900,000.

The commercial bank will record the loan repayment of $100,000 in the same manner it records all loan repayments, i.e. by simultaneously reducing the loan and the deposit. Since the deposits have been replaced by the entry called National Credit, the National Credit is reduced. The result is below:

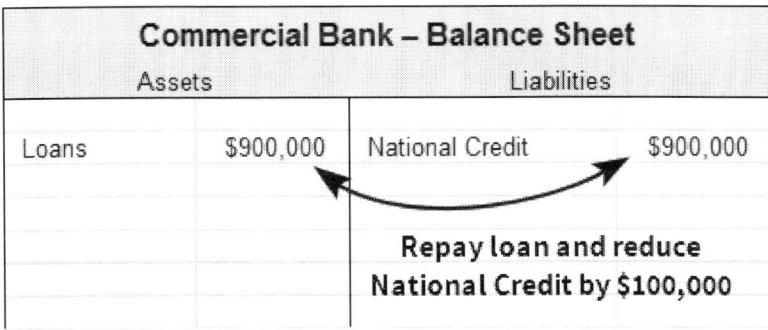

The reduction of $100,000 in National Credit is recorded simultaneous with the creation of new money by the independent monetary authority (as detailed below). The reduction is a record of the fact that the government has accessed part of the seigniorage owed to Australia. The remaining balance of $900,000 is the future benefit yet to be received.

Fast route: Money creation

The independent monetary authority will create $100,000 and deposit the money into the account of the government at the RBA Currency Trust Fund. The money will be spent on infrastructure.

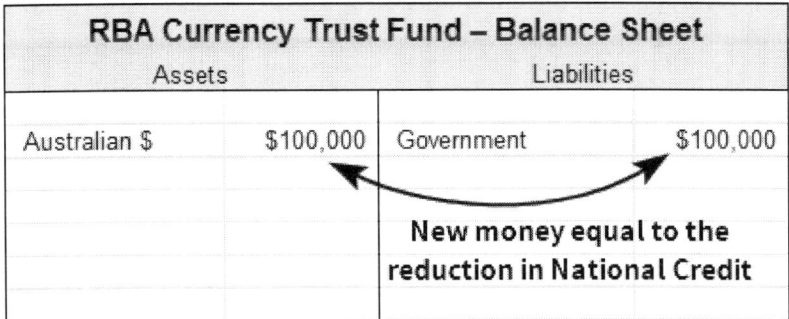

The total money supply is now restored back to $1 million.

Seigniorage and value

The major difference between the routes is the speed with which deposits are moved to currency trust funds. Both routes generate the same amount of seigniorage for the government. Neither route is expected to accelerate or retard the receipt of such seigniorage (as existing bank loans are repaid).

One benefit of the fast route is a significant reduction in the probability of bank runs and bail-ins. With all deposits held at currency trust funds, their value is no longer determined by commercial bank assets, such as loans or complex derivative products. Historically, bank assets can be devalued dramatically – as evidenced in the global financial crisis of 2008.

Banking services

The Fair Money solution restrains commercial banks from monetising debt. As their balance sheets are wound down, it is expected that they will create a number of currency trust funds where they act as trustees. Since banks have their own cash resources, they are expected to lend their own funds in order to generate additional revenue.

Currency trust funds provide **true banking services,** since they act as intermediaries between lenders and borrowers. Currently, commercial banks are not intermediaries since they do not lend client deposits.

Many of the services that commercial banks currently provide will continue to be rendered. For example:

- Collection on existing loans.
- Credit assessments.
- Property related services.
- Insurance related services.
- Payment infrastructure.
- Buying and selling foreign exchange.
- Creating investment products.

The introduction of currency trust funds is expected to stimulate new financial services and products, for which the banks (acting as trustees) will be remunerated.

Creative opportunity

Abraham Lincoln called the process whereby money is created by the government, the greatest creative opportunity of government. His statement on the subject is below:

> The privilege of **creating and issuing money** is not only the supreme prerogative of Government, but it is the Government's **greatest creative opportunity... The taxpayers will be saved immense sums of interest,** discounts and exchanges. The financing of all **public enterprises**, the maintenance of stable government and ordered progress, and the conduct of the Treasury will become matters of practical administration.

The Fair Money solution differs only slightly from the approach articulated by Abraham Lincoln. The Fair Money solution advocates that an independent body, out of reach of politicians, measure and create the national currency and then place it at the disposal of the government to be spent on public infrastructure.

Measure the benefit

As at September 2016, approximately $1.83 trillion of digital money had been created in Australia by commercial banks via debt monetisation.

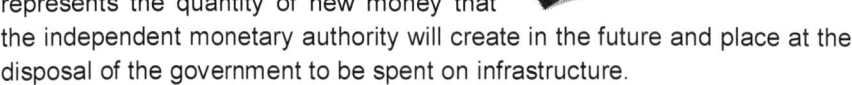

Under the Fair Money solution, this figure represents the quantity of new money that the independent monetary authority will create in the future and place at the disposal of the government to be spent on infrastructure.

Since the money no longer needs to be obtained via taxation, it represents a tax saving. Estimating the annual benefit is dependent on the repayment of existing commercial bank loans. For example, if all commercial bank loans (created via debt monetisation) are repaid over 15 years, then the average annual financial benefit is:

$$\$122 \text{ billion annually} = \frac{\$1.83 \text{ trillion (commercial bank money)}}{15}$$

This amount of money is significant when compared to the annual budget of the Australian federal government.

Debt is slavery

A transition from a debt-based monetary system to an asset-based monetary system is not beyond the capacity of a government that has the interests of its residents at heart. As the transition progresses, the probability of bank runs and bank bail-ins diminish. The end result is a reduction in taxes and a reduction in both private and public debt.

Parents have a moral obligation to bequeath to their children a better environment and a world that is free of debt. Debt is an invisible shackle that restricts the action of those that carry its burden. Our collective narcissism has allowed us to live a better life at the expense of future generations. Our children deserve better, and we certainly should know better.

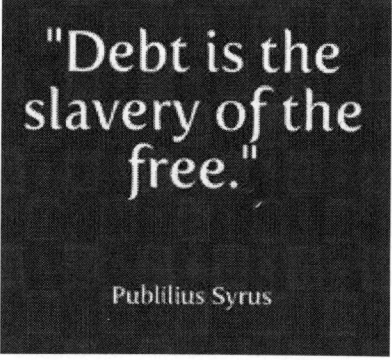

"Debt is the slavery of the free."

Publilius Syrus

Chapter 27 :   Extra topics

Banks lend by creating credit. They create the means of payment out of nothing.

Sir Ralph George Hawtrey (1879 - 1975)
former Secretary to the UK Treasury

Nationalise banks

Commercial banks practice debt monetisation, and pay dividends to their shareholders. The objectionable part of our debt-based monetary system is not who the shareholders of the commercial banks are, but the practice of debt monetisation.

Many proponents of alternate monetary systems suggest that by nationalising commercial banks, our financial woes will be cured. This course of action is akin to declaring that if the government becomes the sole recipient of plunder, then the practice of plunder should be tolerated. The mind boggles.

Communism

The Fair Money solution displays superficial features of communism. To examine the issue we turn to the 5th plank of the Communist Manifesto:

> Centralization of credit in the hands of the state, by means of a national bank with State capital and an exclusive monopoly.

The various components are addressed below:

National bank: The Fair Money solution does not propose the creation of a national bank. The business of banking (i.e. of being an intermediary between lender and borrower) is best practiced by the free market. The function of the independent monetary authority is limited to measuring and controlling the quantity of the national currency in circulation.

Credit: The term implies that money is lent and that it must be repaid. The Fair Money solution states that the independent monetary authority should create the national currency and place it at the disposal of government – without any expectation of repayment.

Credit in the hands of the state: The term implies that the state should own all banks, and that they continue their practise of debt monetisation. The Fair Money solution is the antithesis of debt monetisation.

Exclusive monopoly: The term implies that there should be no competition to the state bank. The Fair Money solution places no restriction on the number of banks or lenders – be they public or private.

Taxes are obsolete

In 1946 the American Affairs journal published a paper that Mr Beardsley Ruml (then chairman of the Federal Reserve Bank of New York) presented to the American Bar Association in 1945. The title of the paper is Taxes for Revenue are Obsolete. The following extract is enlightening:

> Final **freedom from the domestic money market** exists for every sovereign national state where there exists an institution which functions in the manner of a modern central bank, and whose **currency is not convertible into gold** or some other commodity.

The paper declares the following sources of government funding to be obsolete (or unnecessary):

- **Taxes** – as stated in the title.
- **Loans** – since "freedom exists from the domestic money market".

If taxes and loans are unnecessary, then one may ask what source of funding is available to government. Mr Ruml points to "an institution which functions in the manner of a modern central bank". Interestingly, Mr Ruml did not say "a central bank". Implied is that a government entity should create the required money.

This has resonance with Article 1 Section 8 of the American Constitution:

> The Congress shall have the power ... **to coin money**, regulate the value thereof, and of foreign coin, and fix the standard of weights and measures;

The term "to coin" is a verb, and in 1776 it was generally applied to indicate that something is created or manufactured. It is not unreasonable to conclude that Mr Beardsley Ruml is alluding to the **unalienable right of government to create the national currency and to spend it into circulation in lieu of taxes**.

Gold as a money class

Gold is an effective store of value in times of economic crisis. During periods of price inflation and hyperinflation, gold has retained its purchasing power relative to physical assets.

The price of gold is a barometer of the health of the currency in which it is quoted. A sustained increase in the price of gold indicates that the underlying currency is being devalued, normally through monetary inflation. Consequently, any investment in precious metals is equivalent to taking out insurance against the debasement of the underlying currency.

The Fair Money solution recognises the benefit of maintaining gold as a distinct money class and a concurrent form of money. Having the freedom to select a medium of exchange and a store of value is evidence of a robust monetary system.

Cyber currencies

Theoretically, alternate currencies such as Bitcoin should be allowed to compete with national currencies. However, there are many aspects of these alternate currencies that make them undesirable, especially when money is considered to be a public utility. If the public were better informed, the calls for the use of such alternate currencies would be more circumspect.

Bitcoin has not only created numerous USD millionaires, but the mythical founder of Bitcoin, Satoshi Nakamoto was recently declared to be a USD billionaire. The financial status of these individuals stems from three factors, namely:

- Their early adoption of Bitcoin.
- Bitcoin limited to 21 million units (i.e. a limited supply).
- The growing public demand for Bitcoin.

People who are technologically challenged find themselves outside the circle of Bitcoin beneficiaries. Money should never favour any particular class – be they early adopters or the technologically astute. Money should serve the rich, the poor, the educated and the illiterate in equal measure, and at all times. As the price of Bitcoin rises, new owners subsidise the lifestyle of the early adopters.

Bitcoin is not immune to bail-ins. In August 2016, Bitfinex (a Bitcoin exchange) announced that they would be confiscating a portion of client deposits. Zerohedge.com stated in part:

> …all of its users will **lose 36% of their deposits** after it concluded its review [of] the massive hack, in what is set to be the first ever Bitcoin **bail-in**.

Imagine the public outcry if a similar statement was made by a commercial bank. Yet, Bitcoin pundits ignore this precedent and continue touting public adoption.

Currency swaps

Up to this point, we have observed how money is created when:

- Commercial banks monetise debt.
- Central banks monetise financial securities.

A third instance exists, and that is where commercial banks enter into currency swaps. A currency swap involves two banks, with each bank operating in a different country. Investopedia defines a currency swap as follows:

> In a currency swap, two parties exchange the **interest and principal of one loan** in one currency for the **interest and principal of another loan** in another currency.

A currency swap consists of two simultaneous loan transactions, where each bank monetises the debt of the other bank. For example, a US based bank enters into a currency swap with an Australian bank:

At the start of the currency swap, the following two transactions occur:

- Bank A monetises the debt of Bank B, and lends US dollars.
- Bank B monetises the debt of Bank A, and lends Australian dollars.

At the end of the swap, both loan transactions are reversed as each bank repays their loan with interest. Currency swaps allow two commercial banks (in different countries) to increase the supply of commercial bank money – without the involvement of the general public.

Global liquidity crisis

During the global financial crisis of 2008, the biggest debt monetisation in history occurred as the Federal Reserve System lent $16 trillion of central bank money to 407 global banks. An audit of the Federal Reserve (the first in almost 100 years) culminated in a report published in September 2012. At the time, the GDP of the United States was approximately $14 trillion.

The top recipients of Federal Reserve lending were:

- Citigroup: $2.5 trillion
- Morgan Stanley: $2.04 trillion
- Merrill Lynch: $1.949 trillion
- Bank of America: $1.344 trillion
- Barclays PLC (United Kingdom): $868 billion
- Bear Sterns: $853 billion
- Goldman Sachs: $814 billion
- Royal Bank of Scotland (UK): $541 billion
- JP Morgan Chase: $391 billion
- Deutsche Bank (Germany): $354 billion
- UBS (Switzerland): $287 billion
- Credit Suisse (Switzerland): $262 billion
- Lehman Brothers: $183 billion
- Bank of Scotland (United Kingdom): $181 billion
- BNP Paribas (France): $175 billion

The quantum of such lending suggests that our monetary system (which is predicated on debt monetisation) is seriously flawed. A viable remedy to this unhealthy state is the Fair Money solution, whose implementation will result in lower private and public debt and a reduction in the probability of bank runs and bail-ins.

Terminology: Make money

The media is awash with terms that mislead the public as to the nature of our monetary system and how it functions.

For example, the term to **make money** is frequently used by the public when discussing their employment or investments. In reality, a limited number of entities make money - as in the creation or manufacture of the Australian dollar. These entities are the central bank, the commercial banks and the various mints (i.e. the Perth Mint and the Royal Australian Mint).

It is more accurate for members of the public to state that they **earn money**, since they exchange their labour for existing money; originally created by a commercial bank via debt monetisation.

 But if thought corrupts language, language can also corrupt thought.

George Orwell
1984

Terminology: Bank liquidity

Another term is **bank liquidity**. The public has a vague notion that it refers to the amount of currency notes held by commercial banks. This is partly true. The Bank of England describes liquid assets in their article Bank Capital and Liquidity published in their Third Quarterly Bulletin 2013:

> As well as loans, [commercial] banks hold a number of other types of assets, including liquid assets such as **cash, central bank reserves or government bonds**.

The extract informs us that liquid assets include:

- Cash (i.e. currency notes and coins).
- Central bank money.
- Government bonds.

The Bank of England continues and discusses liquidity risk.

> Liquidity risk takes on a number of forms. Primarily for a [commercial] bank, it is the risk that a large number of depositors and investors may **withdraw their savings**...

Depositors can withdraw their money in the form of currency notes or by way of transferring their account balance to another commercial bank.

Commercial banks obtain currency notes by purchasing them from the central bank and paying with central bank money. When depositors transfer their account balance to another bank, the commercial bank needs to have sufficient central bank money.

The common denominator is central bank money. Consequently, **bank liquidity** refers primarily to the amount of central bank money that commercial banks hold.

Comparison

A short comparison of three monetary systems is provided below.

	Current system	Gold standard	Fair Money
Based on	Debt	Gold	Public assets
Debt is	Perpetual	-	Low
Tax is	High	-	Low
Inflation	5.2% pa [1]	-15% to 23% pa [2]	Zero

[1] *Average inflation between 1966 and 2016 (source RBA)*
[2] *Inflation in the USA, The Atlantic 26 August 2012*

Current system

Our current monetary system is based on debt. In order for commercial bank money to exist it has to be borrowed into circulation. Perpetual debt is a hallmark of this system, with taxes increasing over the decades to service public debt. A phrase that best describes our current monetary system is; **in order for money to exist – debt has to be incurred**.

Gold standard

A phrase that best describes the gold standard is; **in order for money to exist – minerals have to be mined**. In the USA, the gold standard endured for approximately 54 years (often cited to be between 1879 and 1933). Contrary to the notion that gold provides economic stability, the two dates bookmark a number of economic disasters, namely:

- The Recession of 1882-85.
- The Panic of 1893.
- The Panic of 1896.
- The Panic of 1907.
- The Panic of 1910-1911.
- The Depression of 1920.
- The Great Depression of 1929.

The Atlantic newspaper of 26 August 2012 provides the following chart of the consumer price index in the USA during the period of the gold standard.

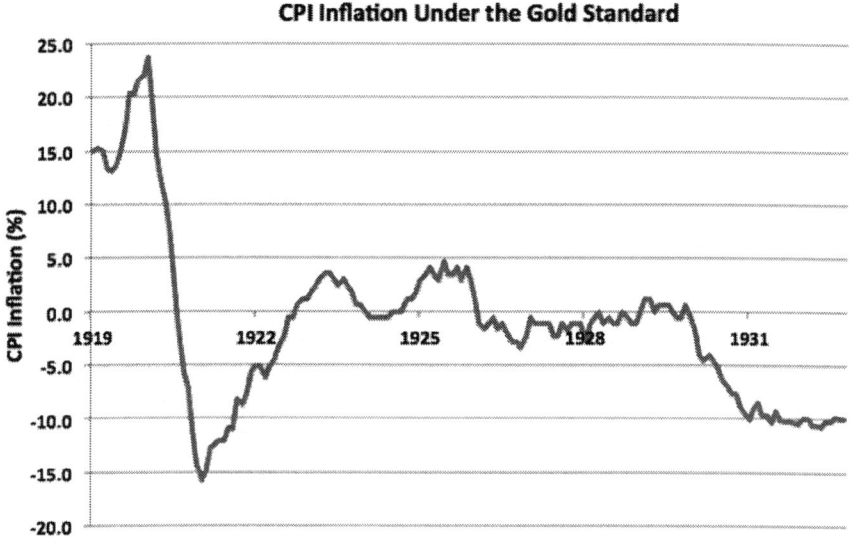

Quantity of gold

The idea of returning to a gold standard has vocal detractors. They point out that there is an insufficient amount of gold to underpin the world money supply. The BBC estimates that there is approximately 171,300 tonnes of gold in the world, i.e. 5.507 billion troy ounces. With the world population at approximately 7.2 billion, it means there is less than an ounce of gold for each person on the earth.

Moreover, Bullionvault.com states that current gold demand is split into the following sectors:

- 60% jewellery.
- 20% investment bars and coins.
- 10% technology.
- 10% central banks.

The question of using precious metals to back the national currency stretches back decades. Abraham Lincoln addressed the issue as below:

 The available supply of gold and silver being wholly inadequate to permit the issuance of coins of intrinsic value or paper currency convertible into coin in the volume required to serve the needs of the people, **some other basis for the issue of currency must be developed....**

Abraham Lincoln
16th President of the United States
March 1861 – April 1865

Return to a gold standard

Jim Rickards is a renowned author, and an advocate of returning to a gold standard. In his article on Dailyreckoning.com.au dated 11 August 2016, he states:

People say there's not enough gold to support the international monetary system. A gold standard sounds good, but the global financial system is so large, there's not enough gold to support the money supply ... As I show in the book [The new case for gold], that's nonsense.

He lists two actions that will allow gold to be used as money. The first is that of setting the price of gold:

All we have to do is **increase the gold price**... gold can always support any amount of money supply if its **price is set properly**... Just take the amount of money supply in the world, and the

> amount of physical gold in the world, divide one by the other, and there's the gold price.

The second is that of backing the money supply with a fraction of gold:

> Do you want the money supply backed 100% by gold, or is 40% sufficient? ... I think **40% is reasonable**.

In summary, Mr Rickards proposes:

- The global money supply should be backed 40% by gold.
- The price of gold should be set according to his formula.

Use of the word "set" screams fiat. Recall that fiat is a term derived from Latin, where it means: **Let it become, it will become** (as in a decree or an order). Furthermore, by backing the money supply with 40% gold means that his proposal has the characteristics of a fractional reserve banking system.

Exorbitant privilege

During the 1960s the term exorbitant privilege was used on the political stage to describe the use of the US dollar as the de facto currency for international trade settlement. The term was coined by the French Minister of Finance, Valéry Giscard d'Estaing and repeated by Charles de Gaulle. It alludes to the unfair  nature of having to use a specific currency when paying for the goods and services from a foreign nation.

The extensive use of the US dollar for international trade settlement has directly benefitted the United States, and particularly their banking sector. The benefit is in the form of interest earned, since the expanded supply of US dollars (i.e. commercial bank money) exists only by virtue of being borrowed into circulation. The remedy is not to declare a different currency as being the better candidate, but to introduce neutrality into international trade settlement. Gold is ideally suit to this role – since it does not favour the nation creating the reserve currency, but only the nation that is industrious and productive.

Fair Money

The Fair Money solution does not attempt to set the price of gold or the price of money (i.e. interest rates). The free market should be the arbiter of price. All price manipulations throughout history have proven to have unintended consequences. The Fair Money solution seeks only to control the quantity of money in circulation, so that price inflation remains at zero (i.e. the value of the currency is preserved).

 Steady state **inflation can drop to zero** without posing problems for the conduct of monetary policy.

> Research Department
> International Monetary Fund
> The Chicago Plan Revisited (page 8)

The Fair Money solution requires the national currency be created by an independent monetary authority, and spent into circulation by the government on public infrastructure (in lieu of taxes). This means that public assets such as roads, hospitals, schools, power stations, dams, bridges, libraries, stadiums, law courts, electrical grids, tunnels, airports, trains, trams etc. can be financed without additional taxes.

A phrase that best describes the Fair Money solution is; **money is created in conjunction with public assets - without debt or additional taxes**.

Sources & publications

The articles and documents that form the basis of this book are sourced from the institutions given below. The web site **fairmoney.info** provides a list of the most important documents, which readers can download for further study.

- The Bank of England.
- The Federal Reserve System.
- The International Monetary Fund.
- The Reserve Bank of Australia.
- KPMG.

Below is a list of independent publications that have added context and colour to this book. They are provided in no particular order:

- The lost science of money - Stephen Zarlenga.
- No more national debt – Bill Still.
- The money masters (DVD) – Bill Still.
- The web of debt - Ellen Hodgson Brown.
- The creature from Jekyll Island – G. Edward Griffin.
- The coming battle – Paul Walter & Lorraine Walter.
- They own it all – Ronald MacDonald & Robert Rowen.
- The secrets of the Federal Reserve – Eustace Mullins.
- Sovereign money – Positive Money.
- All about the money (DVD) – Positive Money.
- Where does money come from – Ryan-Collins, Greenham et al.
- Modernising money – Andrew Jackson & Ben Dyson
- Modern money secrets – Byron Dale.
- Fiat paper money – Ralph T. Foster.
- Money creation – E. L. Burgi.
- Financial terrorism – John F. McManus.
- A matter of life or debt – Eric de Maré.
- The money trick – unknown author (Veritas Publishing).
- Billions for the bankers, debts for the people – Sheldon Emry.

Chapter 28 : Summary

History will have to record that the greatest tragedy of this period of social transition was not the strident clamour of the bad people, but the appalling silence of the good people.

Martin Luther King, Jr.

Longevity

The longevity of our debt-based monetary system is a marvel. A possible reason is recorded in the correspondence of the Rothschild brothers of London to their associates in New York in 1863:

> The few who understand the system will either be **so interested in its profits** or be so dependent upon its favours that there will be no opposition from that class, while on the other hand, the great body of people, mentally incapable of comprehending the tremendous advantage that capital derives from the system, will bear its burdens without complaint, and perhaps **without even suspecting that the system is inimical to their interests**.

Another view on the subject is provided by the economist Frederic Bastiat:

 When plunder becomes a way of life for a group of men living together in society, they create for themselves in the course of time a legal system that authorizes it and a moral code that glorifies it.

Frederic Bastiat
30 June 1801 - 24 December 1850
French political economist

Final comment

Our current monetary system operates on the basis that in order for commercial bank money to exist – it has to be borrowed into existence. With the application of interest, the cumulative debt becomes impossible to repay with existing money. The result is perpetual debt and the transfer of physical wealth.

The Fair Money solution is a simple and fair alternative. It lifts the burden of debt, and benefits both government and the public. As Mandela stated;

> **"Poverty is not an accident... it is man-made and can be removed by the actions of human beings."**

Final thought

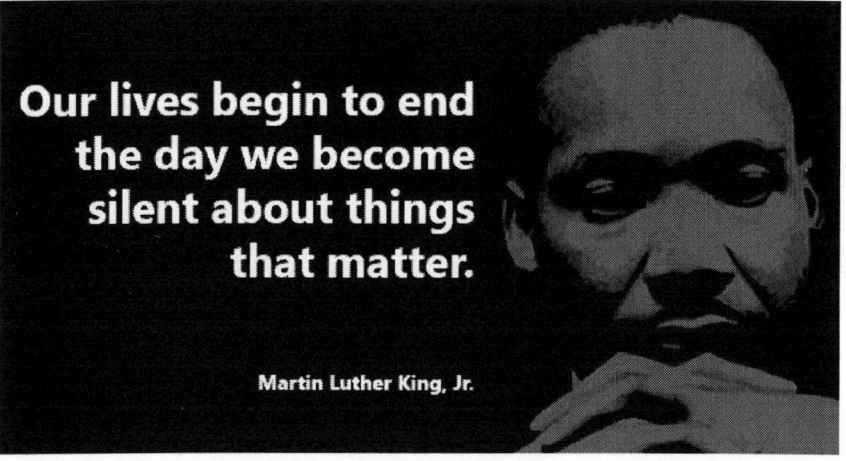

Our lives begin to end the day we become silent about things that matter.

Martin Luther King, Jr.

Speak out.

== The End ==

Printed in Great Britain
by Amazon

54527048R00126